Random House Webster's

Pocket Rhyming Dictionary

Second Edition

Random House
Webster's
Pocket
Rhyming
Dictionary

Second Edition

RANDOM HOUSE
NEW YORK

Random House Webster's
Pocket Rhyming Dictionary, Second Edition

This is a revised edition of a work originally published in 1960 as *The Random House Rhyming Dictionary.*

Trademarks
A number of entered words which we have reason to believe constitute trademarks have been designated as such. However, no attempt has been made to designate as trademarks or service marks all terms or words in which proprietary rights might exist. The inclusion, exclusion, or definition of a word or term is not intended to affect, or to express a judgment on, the validity or legal status of the word or term as a trademark, service mark, or other proprietary term.

Library of Congress Cataloging-in-Publication Number: 98-68645

This book is available for special purchases in bulk by organizations and institutions, not for resale, at special discounts. Please direct your inquiries to the Random House Special Sales Department, toll-free 888-591-1200 or fax 212-572-4961.

Please address inquiries about electronic licensing of this division's products, for use on a network or in software or on CD-ROM, to the Subsidiary Rights Department, Random House Reference & Information Publishing, fax 212-940-7370.

Typeset and printed in the United States of America.

Visit the Random House Web site at www.randomhouse.com

Second Edition
0 9 8 7 6 5 4 3 2 1
4/99
ISBN: 0-375-70514-7

New York   Toronto   London   Sydney   Auckland

Contents

Staff

Editor, second edition: Georgia S. Maas
Editor, first edition: Jess Stein
Support Staff: Annette Apitz, Nancy Armstrong, Michael Lewis, Amy Warner
Editorial Production Services: Jennifer Dowling, Seaside Press
Production Editor: Joseph W. Sora
Database Associate: Diane M. João
Database Manager: Constance A. Baboukis
Director of Production: Patricia W. Ehresmann
Managing Editor: Andrew Ambraziejus
Editorial Director: Wendalyn Nichols
Associate Publisher: Page Edmunds
Publisher: Charles M. Levine

Preface

The Second Edition of the *Random House Webster's Pocket Rhyming Dictionary* offers writers of songs and poetry more than 30,000 words in a compact, easy-to-use format. The rhyming words encompass common vocabulary, foreign expressions, and proper names, including place names and many names from literature and mythology. Terms that have entered the language during the past decade have been added to bring the book up to date. A number of words that are rare or obsolete have been included to offer writers possibilities that might not come readily to mind.

Rhyming words for the final syllable are given in one list, and rhymes for the final two syllables in another list. These rhyming words have been placed under the most common spelling for a particular sound, while abundant cross references help the user find rhymes for different spellings of the same sound. Pronunciations are given for syllables that can be pronounced in more than one way.

In the back of the Dictionary is a glossary of poetic terms that serves as a handy guide to rhyming patterns, making *Random House Webster's Pocket Rhyming Dictionary* the perfect bring-anywhere reference for whenever the muse strikes.

Pronunciation Key

a	act, bat	o͝o	book, put
ā	able, cape	o͞o	ooze, rule
â	air, dare	ou	out, loud
ä	art, calm		
		p	page, stop
b	back, rub	r	read, cry
ch	chief, beach	s	see, miss
d	do, bed	sh	shoe, push
		t	ten, bit
		th	thin, path
e	ebb, set	t͟h	that, other
ē	equal, bee		
f	fit, puff	u	up, love
g	give, beg	yo͞o	use, cute
h	hit, hear	û	urge, burn
		v	voice, live
		w	west, away
i	if, big	y	yes, young
ī	ice, bite	z	zeal, lazy, those
		zh	vision, measure
j	just, edge	ə	occurs only in unac-
k	kept, make		cented syllables and in-
l	low, all		dicates the sound of
			a *in* along
m	my, him		e *in* system
n	now, on		i *in* easily
ng	sing, England		o *in* gallop
			u *in* circus
o	box, hot		
ō	over, no	ᵊ	used between *i* and *r*
ô	order, ball		and between *ou* and *r*
oi	oil, joy		to show triphthongal
			quality, as in *fire* (fīᵊr),
			hour (ouᵊr)

One-Syllable Rhymes

-a (-ä), ah, baa, bah, blah, bra, fa, froid, ha, ja, la, ma, pa, pas, Ra, shah, spa; à bas, bourgeois, Degas, éclat, état, faux pas, grandma, grandpa, hurrah, huzza, mama, papa, pasha, pasta, Utah, viva, voilà; agora, baccarat, cha cha cha, coup d'état, la-di-da, Mardi Gras, Modena, moussaka, Omaha, Ottawa, panama, Panama, Shangri-la; Ali Baba, ayatollah, Caligula, cucaracha, hors de combat, je ne sais quoi, ménage à trois, res publica, utopia; Tegucigalpa; funiculi-funicula.

-a (-ā). See **-ay.**

-ab, bab, blab, cab, crab, dab, drab, gab, grab, jab, Mab, nab, scab, slab, stab, tab; Ahab, bedab, Joab, Moab, Punjab, Skylab; baobab, taxicab.

-abe, Abe, babe, nabe; astrolabe.

-ac. See **-ack.**

-ace, ace, base, bass, brace, case, chase, dace, face, grace, Grace, lace, mace, pace, place, plaice, race, space, Thrace, trace, vase; abase, apace, birthplace, briefcase, debase, deface, disgrace, displace, efface, embrace, encase, erase, grimace, horserace, misplace, outface, outpace, replace, retrace, staircase, ukase, uncase, unlace; about-face, aerospace, carapace, commonplace, contrabass, funnyface, interlace, interspace, marketplace, outer space, steeplechase.

-aced. See **-aste.**

-ach (-ak). See **-ack**.

-ach (-ach). See **-atch**.

-ache (-āk). See **-ake**.

-ache (-ash). See **-ash**.

-acht, (-ät). See **-ot**.

-ack, back, black, clack, claque, crack, hack, jack, Jack, knack, lac, lack, Mac, pack, plaque, quack, rack, sac, sack, sacque, shack, slack, smack, snack, stack, tack, thwack, track, whack, wrack, yak; aback, ack-ack, alack, arrack, attack, bareback, bivouac, blackjack, bootblack, cognac, drawback, gimcrack, haystack, hogback, horseback, humpback, hunchback, Iraq, kayak, Kodak, knickknack, macaque, Meshach, Muzak, Prozac, ransack, repack, rucksack, Shadrach, shellac, Slovak, ticktack, unpack, zweiback; almanac, amphibrach, applejack, bric-a-brac, Cadillac, cardiac, cul-de-sac, Fond du Lac, Frontenac, Hackensack, hackmatack, haversack, iliac, ipecac, maniac, pickaback, piggyback, Pontiac, stickleback, tamarack, umiak, zodiac; ammoniac, demoniac, elegiac, symposiac; aphrodisiac, dipsomaniac, hypochondriac, kleptomaniac, pyromaniac, sacroiliac.

-acked. See **-act**.

-acks. See **-ax**.

-act, bract, fact, pact, tact, tract; abstract, attract, compact, contact, contract, detract, diffract, distract, enact, entr'acte, exact, extract, impact, infract, intact, protract, react, redact, refract, retract, subtract, transact; abreact, artifact, cataract, counteract, interact, overact, re-enact, retroact, subcom-

pact, underact; matter-of-fact, overreact.
   Also: **-ack** + **-ed** (as in *packed, attacked*, etc.)

-ad (-ad), ad, add, bad, bade, brad, cad, Chad, clad, dad, fad, gad, glad, had, lad, mad, pad, plaid, sad, scad, shad, tad; Baghdad, dryad, footpad, forbade, gonad, monad, naiad, nomad, Pleiad, Sinbad, tetrad, unclad; aoudad, deadbeat dad, Dunciad, Galahad, hebdomad, Iliad, ironclad, Trinidad, undergrad; olympiad.

-ad (-od). See **-od.**

-ade, aid, bade, blade, braid, cade, fade, glade, grade, jade, lade, laid, made, maid, neighed, paid, raid, shade, spade, staid, suede, they'd, trade, wade; abrade, afraid, alcaide, arcade, Band-Aid, Belgrade, blockade, brigade, brocade, cascade, charade, cockade, crusade, degrade, dissuade, evade, grenade, homemade, housemaid, invade, limeade, mermaid, nightshade, parade, persuade, pervade, pomade, postpaid, prepaid, self-made, stockade, tirade, unmade, unpaid, upbraid; accolade, Adelaide, ambuscade, balustrade, barricade, cannonade, cavalcade, centigrade, chambermaid, colonnade, custom-made, enfilade, escalade, escapade, esplanade, fusillade, gallopade, gasconade, lemonade, marinade, marmalade, masquerade, orangeade, overlaid, palisade, plantigrade, promenade, ready-made, renegade, retrograde, serenade, underpaid; harlequinade, rodomontade.
   Also: **-ay** + **-ed** (as in *played,* etc.)

Also: **-eigh** + **-ed** (as in *weighed*, etc.)
Also: **-ey** + **-ed** (as in *preyed*, etc.)

-ade (-ād). See **-ad.**

-ade (-od). See **-od.**

-adge, badge, cadge, hajj, Madge.

-afe, chafe, safe, strafe, waif; fail-safe, unsafe, vouchsafe.

-aff, calf, chaff, gaff, graph, half, laugh, quaff, staff; behalf, carafe, distaff, Falstaff, flagstaff, giraffe, horselaugh, pikestaff, riffraff, seraph; autograph, cenotaph, epitaph, half-and-half, lithograph, monograph, paragraph, phonograph, photograph, polygraph, quarterstaff, shandygaff, telegraph. See also **-off.**

-affed. See **-aft.**

-aft, aft, craft, daft, draft, draught, graft, haft, kraft, laughed, raft, shaft, Taft, waft; abaft, aircraft, ingraft, seacraft, spacecraft, stagecraft, statecraft, witchcraft; handicraft, overdraft, watercraft.

Also: **-aff** + **-ed** (as in *staffed*, etc.)
Also: **-aph** + **-ed** (as in *autographed*, etc.)

-ag, bag, brag, crag, drag, fag, flag, gag, hag, jag, lag, nag, quag, rag, sag, scrag, shag, slag, snag, stag, swag, tag, wag; dishrag, grabbag, ragtag, sandbag, wigwag, zigzag; Brobdingnag, bullyrag, saddlebag, scalawag.

-age (-āj), age, cage, gage, gauge, page, rage, sage, stage, swage, wage; assuage, backstage, birdcage, engage, enrage, front page, greengage, outrage, presage, space age, teenage; disengage, overage, underage.

-age (-ij), bridge, midge, ridge; abridge, Cambridge, drawbridge, footbridge, pillage, village; acreage, anchorage, appanage, arbitrage, average, beverage, brokerage, cartilage, cozenage, equipage, factorage, foliage, fuselage, hemorrhage, heritage, hermitage, lineage, mucilage, overage, parentage, parsonage, pasturage, patronage, personage, pilgrimage, privilege, reportage, sacrilege, sortilege, tutelage, vicarage.

-age (-äzh), barrage, collage, corsage, garage, gavage, ménage, mirage, moulage; arbitrage, badinage, bon voyage, camouflage, curettage, decoupage, entourage, fuselage, Hermitage, persiflage, reportage; espionage.

-agm. See **-am.**

-agne. See **-ain.**

-ague, Hague, plague, vague; fainaigue.

-ah. See **-a.**

-aid (-ād). See **-ade.**

-aid (-ed). See **-ed.**

-aif. See **-afe.**

-aight. See **-ate.**

-aign. See **-ain.**

-ail, ail, ale, bail, bale, Braille, dale, Dale, fail, flail, frail, Gael, Gail, gale, gaol, grail, hail, hale, jail, kale, mail, male, nail, pail, pale, quail, Quayle, rail, sail, sale, scale, shale, snail, stale, swale, tail, tale, they'll, trail, vale, veil, wail, wale, whale, Yale; assail, avail, bewail, bobtail, cocktail, curtail, detail, dovetail, entail, exhale, fantail, female, hobnail, impale, inhale, prevail, regale, retail, travail, unveil, wassail, wholesale; abigail, Abigail, Bloomingdale, countervail, farthingale, ginger ale, Holy Grail, martingale, monorail, nightingale, ponytail, triticale.

-ails. See **-ales.**

-aim. See **-ame.**

-ain (-ān), Aisne, bane, blain, brain, Cain, cane, chain, crane, Dane, deign, drain, fain, fane, feign, gain, grain, Jane, lain, lane, main, Maine, mane, pain, pane, plain, plane, rain, reign, rein, sane, seine, Shane, skein, slain, Spain, sprain, stain, strain, swain, ta'en, thane, thegn, train, twain, vain, vane, vein, wain, wane, Zane; abstain, again, airplane, amain, arcane, arraign, attain, biplane, campaign, champagne, Champlain, chicane, chilblain, chow mein, cocaine, complain, constrain, contain, demesne, detain, disdain, distrain, dogbane, domain, Duquesne, Elaine, enchain, entrain, ethane, explain, Gawain, germane, henbane, humane, Hussein, inane, insane, Lorraine, maintain, marchpane, membrane, methane, migraine, moraine, murrain, obtain, ordain, pertain, plantain, procaine, profane, ptomaine, quatrain, refrain, regain, remain, restrain, retain, Sinn Fein, sustain, terrain, Ukraine, urbane; aeroplane, appertain, ascertain, cellophane, chamberlain, Charlemagne, chatelaine, counterpane, entertain, frangipane, hurricane, hydroplane, monoplane, porcelain, scatterbrain, weather vane, windowpane; legerdemain.

-ain (-en). See **-en.**

-ainst, 'gainst; against.
    Also: **-ence** + **-ed** (as in *fenced,* etc.)
    Also: **-ense** + **-ed** (as in *condensed,* etc.)
-aint, ain't, faint, feint, mayn't, paint, plaint, quaint, saint, taint; acquaint, attaint, complaint, constraint, distraint, Geraint, greasepaint, restraint.
-aipse, traipse; jackanapes.
    Also: **-ape** + **-s** (as in *grapes,* etc.)
-air. See **-are.**
-aire. See **-are.**
-aired, aired, haired, laird, merde; long-haired, prepared, short-haired, unpaired, unshared; golden-haired.
-airn, bairn, cairn.
-airs. See **-ares.**
-aise (-āz). See **-aze.**
-aise (-ez). See **-ez.**
-ait. See **-ate.**
-aith, eighth, faith, Faith, wraith; interfaith.
-aize. See **-aze.**
-ak. See **-ack.**
-ake, ache, bake, Blake, brake, break, cake, crake, drake, fake, flake, hake, Jake, lake, make, quake, rake, sake, shake, slake, snake, spake, stake, steak, strake, take, wake; awake, backache, bespake, betake, cornflake, daybreak, earache, earthquake, forsake, heartbreak, keepsake, mandrake, mistake, namesake, opaque, outbreak, partake, retake, snowflake, sweepstake, toothache; bellyache, johnnycake, overtake, patty-cake, rattlesnake, stomachache, undertake, wedding cake.

-al, Al, Hal, pal, sal, shall; banal, cabal, ca-
nal, corral, locale, morale, Natal, timbale;
bacchanal, falderal, femme fatale, musi-
cale, pastorale, rationale; Guadalcanal.

-ald, bald, scald; piebald, so-called; Archi-
bald.
>   Also: **-all** + **-ed** (as in *stalled*, etc.)
>   Also: **-aul** + **-ed** (as in *hauled*, etc.)
>   Also: **-awl** + **-ed** (as in *crawled*, etc.)

-ale (-āl). See **-ail.**

-ale (-al). See **-al.**

-ales, Wales; entrails, marseilles, Marseilles.
>   Also: **-ail** + **-s** (as in *fails*, etc.)
>   Also: **-ale** + **-s** (as in *scales*, etc.)

-alf. See **-aff.**

-alk, auk, balk, calk, chalk, gawk, hawk,
squawk, stalk, talk, walk; Bartok, board-
walk, catwalk, Mohawk; belle epoque,
double talk, tomahawk; Manitowoc;
Oconomowoc.

-all (-al). See **-al.**

-all (-ôl). See **-awl.**

-alled. See **-ald.**

-alm, alm, balm, calm, Guam, palm, psalm,
qualm; becalm, embalm, madame, salaam.

-alp, alp, Alp, palp, scalp.

-alt (-ôlt), fault, halt, malt, salt, smalt, vault;
asphalt, assault, basalt, cobalt, default, ex-
alt; somersault.

-alt (-alt), alt, shalt.

-alts. See **-altz.**

-altz, waltz.
>   Also: **-alt** + **-s** (as in *salts*, etc.)
>   Also: **-ault** + **-s** (as in *faults*, etc.)

-alve (-av), calve, halve, have, salve, Slav;
Yugoslav.

-alve (-äv), calve, Graves, halve, salve, Slav,
suave, Zouave.

-alve (-alv), salve, valve; bivalve; univalve.

-am, am, cam, Cham, clam, cram, dam,
damn, drachm, dram, gram, ham, jam,
jamb, lam, lamb, ma'am, Pam, pram, ram,
RAM, Sam, scram, sham, slam, swam,
tram, wham, yam; Assam, Edam, exam,
flimflam, Graham, iamb, logjam, madame,
Priam, program, Siam; Abraham, aero-
gram, Alabam, Amsterdam, Birmingham,
anagram, cablegram, cryptogram, diagram,
diaphragm, dithyramb, epigram, hexagram,
marjoram, monogram, Rotterdam, Suri-
nam, telegram; ad nauseam, radiogram;
parallelogram.

-amb. See **-am.**

-ame, aim, blame, came, claim, dame, fame,
flame, frame, game, lame, maim, Mame,
name, same, shame, tame; acclaim,
aflame, became, beldame, declaim, de-
fame, disclaim, exclaim, inflame, misname,
nickname, proclaim, reclaim, surname;
overcame.

-amp (-amp), amp, camp, champ, clamp,
cramp, damp, guimpe, lamp, ramp, scamp,
stamp, tamp, tramp, vamp; decamp, en-
camp, firedamp, revamp; afterdamp.

-amp (-omp). See **-omp.**

-an (-an), an, Ann, Anne, ban, bran, can,
clan, Dan, fan, Fran, Jan, Klan, man, Nan,
pan, Pan, plan, ran, scan, span, tan, than,
van; afghan, Afghan, began, corban, dish-

pan, divan, fantan, foreran, he-man, Iran, japan, Japan, Koran, Milan, pavan, pecan, rattan, sedan, trepan, unman; Alcoran, artisan, astrakhan, Astrakhan, caravan, catalan, courtesan, Hindustan, Kazakhstan, Kyrgyzstan, middleman, minuteman, overran, Pakistan, Parmesan, partisan, Peter Pan, spick-and-span, Turkestan, Yucatan; Afghanistan, catamaran, orangutan, Turkmenistan, Uzbekistan.

-an (-on). See **-on.**

-ance (-ans), chance, dance, France, glance, hanse, lance, manse, pants, prance, stance, trance; advance, askance, bechance, enhance, entrance, expanse, finance, mischance, Penzance, perchance, romance; circumstance.

Also: **-ant** + **-s** (as in *grants*, etc.)

-ance (-äns), Provence, séance; ambience, Liederkranz, renaissance; insouciance, par excellence.

-anch, blanch, Blanche, branch, ganch, ranch, stanch; carte blanche; avalanche.

-anct, sacrosanct.

Also: **-ank** + **-ed** (as in *spanked,* etc.)

-and (-and), and, band, bland, brand, gland, grand, hand, land, rand, sand, stand, strand, Strand; backhand, command, demand, disband, dreamland, expand, forehand, grandstand, Greenland, Iceland, remand, Rhineland, Streisand, unhand, withstand; ampersand, contraband, countermand, fairyland, fatherland, firebrand, four-in-hand, hinterland, Holy Land, Houyhnhnmland, overland, reprimand, Rio

Grande, Samarkand, saraband, underhand, understand, wonderland; misunderstand, multiplicand, Witwatersrand.

    Also: **-an** + **-ed** (as in *banned*, etc.)

-and (-ond). See **-ond**.

-ane. See **-ain**.

-ang, bang, bhang, clang, fang, gang, gangue, hang, pang, rang, sang, slang, sprang, stang, tang, twang, whang, yang; harangue, meringue, mustang, Penang, shebang; boomerang, yin and yang; orangutang.

-ange, change, grange, mange, range, strange; arrange, derange, estrange, exchange; disarrange, interchange, rearrange.

-angue. See **-ang**.

-ank, bank, blank, clank, crank, dank, drank, flank, franc, frank, Frank, hank, Hank, lank, plank, prank, rank, sank, shank, shrank, spank, stank, swank, tank, thank, yank, Yank; embank, outflank, outrank, pointblank, snowbank; mountebank.

-anked. See **-anct**.

-anned. See **-and**.

-anse. See **-ance**.

-ant (-ant), ant, aunt, can't, cant, chant, grant, Grant, Kant, pant, plant, rant, scant, shan't, slant; aslant, decant, descant, displant, enchant, extant, gallant, implant, Levant, recant, supplant, transplant; adamant, commandant, disenchant, gallivant; hierophant.

-ant (-änt), beurre blanc, croissant, savant; en passant, Maupassant; au courant, contretemps, dénouement, en passant, soi dis-

ant, vol-au-vent; accouchement, rapproche-
ment; arrondissement, idiot savant.
-ant. (-ont) See **-aunt.**
-ants. See **-ance.**
-ap, cap, chap, clap, flap, gap, hap, Jap, lap,
map, nap, pap, rap, sap, scrap, slap, snap,
strap, tap, trap, wrap, yap; ASAP, back-
slap, burlap, catnap, claptrap, dunce cap,
entrap, enwrap, foolscap, kidnap, madcap,
mayhap, mishap, nightcap, shrink-wrap,
skullcap, skycap, snowcap, unwrap; after-
clap, handicap, killer app; overlap, rattle-
trap, thunderclap.
-ape, ape, cape, chape, crepe, drape, grape,
jape, nape, rape, scrape, shape, tape;
agape, escape, landscape, moonscape, sea-
scape, shipshape, undrape; audiotape, vid-
eotape.
-apes. See **-aipse.**
-aph. See **-aff.**
-aphed. See **-aft.**
-apped. See **-apt.**
-aps. See **-apse.**
-apse, apse, craps, lapse, schnapps, taps;
collapse, elapse, perhaps, relapse, synapse,
time-lapse.
　　Also: **-ap** + **-s** (as in *claps*, etc.)
-apt, apt, rapt, wrapt; adapt.
　　Also: **-ap** + **-ed** (as in *clapped*, etc.)
-aque. See **-ack.**
-ar (-är), Aar, are, bar, car, char, czar, far,
jar, Loire, mar, par, parr, Saar, scar, spar,
star, tar, tsar; afar, agar, ajar, all-star, ar-
moire, bazaar, bizarre, catarrh, cigar, cou-
loir, Dakar, debar, disbar, felspar, guitar,

horsecar, hussar, lascar, Navarre, pourboire; Alcazar, au revoir, avatar, Balthazar, bête noire, caviar, cinnabar, registrar, rent-a-car, repertoire, reservoir, samovar, seminar, superstar, VCR, Zanzibar; agar-agar.

-ar (-ôr). See **-or.**

-arb, barb, garb; rhubarb.

-arce. See **-arse.**

-arch, arch, larch, march, March, parch, starch; outmarch; countermarch.

-arch. See **-ark.**

-ard (-ärd), bard, card, chard, guard, hard, lard, nard, pard, sard, shard, yard; Bernard, bombard, canard, discard, foulard, Gerard, ill-starred, lifeguard, mallard, midgard, petard, placard, regard, retard, vanguard; Abelard, avant-garde, bodyguard, boulevard, disregard, Hildegarde, interlard, Kierkegaard, leotard, Saint Bernard, Savoyard; camelopard.

Also: **-ar** + **-ed** (as in *starred*, etc.)

-ard (-ôrd). See **-ord.**

-are, air, Ayr, bare, bear, blare, care, chair, Claire, dare, e'er, ere, fair, fare, flair, flare, gare, glair, glare, hair, hare, heir, herr, lair, mare, mayor, ne'er, pair, pare, pear, Pierre, prayer, rare, scare, share, snare, spare, square, stair, stare, swear, tare, tear, their, there, they're, ware, wear, where, yare; affair, armchair, au pair, aware, beware, coheir, compare, corsair, declare, despair, eclair, elsewhere, ensnare, fanfare, forbear, forswear, Gruyère, horsehair, howe'er, impair, mohair, Mynheer, nightmare, outstare, Pierre, prepare, repair, unfair, Voltaire, welfare, whate'er, whene'er, where'er; anywhere, billionaire, Camembert, croix de guerre, debonair, Delaware, doctrinaire, earthenware, étagère, everywhere, Frigidaire, laissez faire, legionnaire, luminaire, maidenhair, mal de mer, millionaire, nom de guerre, outerwear, portecochere, questionnaire, savoir faire, solitaire, thoroughfare, unaware, underwear; chemin de fer, concessionaire, pied-à-terre, son et lumière, vin ordinaire.

-ares, theirs; downstairs, upstairs; unawares.
> Also: **-air** + **-s** (as in *stairs,* etc.)
> Also: **-are** + **-s** (as in *dares,* etc.)
> Also: **-ear** + **-s** (as in *swears,* etc.)
> Also: **-eir** + **-s** (as in *heirs,* etc.)

-arf (-ärf), barf, scarf.

-arf (-ôrf). See **-orf.**

-arge, barge, charge, large, marge, Marge, sarge; discharge, enlarge, recharge, surcharge; overcharge, supercharge, undercharge.

-ark, arc, ark, bark, barque, cark, Clark, dark, hark, lark, mark, Mark, marque, park, sark, shark, snark, spark, stark; aardvark, Bismarck, debark, embark, landmark, Petrarch, remark, skylark, tanbark, trademark; disembark, hierarch, matriarch, meadowlark, oligarch, patriarch.

-arl, carl, Carl, gnarl, marl, snarl.

-arm (-ärm), arm, barm, charm, farm, harm, marm; alarm, disarm, forearm, gendarme, schoolmarm, strong-arm, unarm.

-arm (-ôrm). See **-orm.**

-arn (-ärn), barn, darn, Marne, tarn, yarn.

-arn (-ôrn). See **-orn.**

-arp (-ärp), carp, harp, scarp, sharp, tarp;
cardsharp, escarp; autoharp, counterscarp,
pericarp.

-arp (-ôrp). See **-orp.**

-arred. See **-ard.**

-arse, farce, parse, sparse.

-arsh, harsh, marsh.

-art (-ärt), art, Bart, cart, chart, dart, hart,
heart, mart, part, smart, start, tart; apart,
depart, Descartes, dispart, impart, out-
smart, pushcart, rampart, sweetheart, up-
start; à la carte, counterpart, heart-to-heart,
Lily Bart.

-art (-ôrt). See **-ort.**

-arth (-ärth), Garth, hearth.

-arth (-ôrth). See **-orth.**

-arts (-ôrts). See **-orts.**

-artz (-ôrts). See **-orts.**

-arve, carve, starve.

-as (-oz), Boz, vase, was; La Paz.

-as (-ä). See **-a.**

-as (-as). See **-ass.**

-ase (-ās). See **-ace.**

-ase (-āz). See **-aze.**

-ased. See **-aste.**

-ash (-ash), ash, bash, brash, cache, cash,
clash, crash, dash, flash, gash, gnash,
hash, lash, mash, Nash, pash, plash, rash,
sash, slash, smash, splash, thrash, trash;
abash, callash, mishmash, moustache, pa-
nache, Wabash; balderdash, calabash, sa-
bretache, succotash.

-ash (-osh), bosh, gosh, gouache, josh, posh,

quash, slosh, squash, swash, wash; apache, awash, galosh, goulash; mackintosh.

-ask, ask, bask, Basque, cask, casque, flask, mask, masque, Pasch, task; unmask.

-asm, chasm, plasm, spasm; orgasm, phantasm, sarcasm; cataplasm, pleonasm, protoplasm; enthusiasm, iconoclasm.

-asp, asp, clasp, gasp, grasp, hasp, rasp; enclasp, unclasp.

-ass, ass, bass, brass, class, crass, gas, glass, grass, lass, mass, pass; alas, Alsace, amass, bluegrass, crevasse, cuirasse, harass, impasse, Madras, morass, paillasse, repass, surpass; demitasse, fiberglass, gallowglass, Hallowmas, hippocras, isinglass, lemongrass, looking glass, middle-class, overpass, sassafras, underpass.

-assed. See **-ast.**

-ast, bast, blast, cast, caste, fast, hast, last, mast, past, vast; aghast, avast, Belfast, bombast, broadcast, contrast, forecast, gymnast, miscast, newscast, outcast, peltast, repast, steadfast; flabbergast, overcast, simulcast, telecast; ecclesiast, enthusiast, iconoclast.

Also: **-ass** + **-ed** (as in *passed*, etc.)

-aste, baste, chaste, haste, paste, taste, waist, waste; distaste, foretaste, unchaste; aftertaste.

Also: **-ace** + **-ed** (as in *placed*, etc.)
Also: **-ase** + **-ed** (as in *chased*, etc.)

-at (-at), at, bat, brat, cat, chat, fat, flat, ghat, gnat, hat, mat, Matt, Nat, pat, Pat, phat, plat, rat, sat, slat, spat, sprat, tat, that, vat; combat, cravat, fiat, muskrat, polecat, whereat, wombat; acrobat, Ararat, autocrat, Automat, bureaucrat, butterfat, caveat, copycat, democrat, diplomat, habitat, hemostat, Kattegat, Montserrat, photostat, plutocrat, thermostat, tit for tat; aristocrat, Jehoshaphat, magnificat.

-at (-ä). See **-a.**

-at (-ot). See **-ot.**

-atch (-ach), batch, catch, hatch, latch, match, patch, scratch, snatch, thatch; attach, detach, dispatch, mismatch, unlatch; bandersnatch.

-atch (-och). See **-otch.**

-ate (-ate), ait, ate, bait, bate, crate, date, eight, fate, fête, frate, freight, gait, gate, grate, great, hate, Kate, late, mate, Nate, pate, plait, plate, prate, rate, sate, skate, slate, spate, state, straight, strait, Tate, trait, wait, weight; abate, aerate, agnate, await, baccate, berate, bookplate, bromate, casemate, castrate, caudate, cerate, checkmate, chelate, chlorate, chromate, cirrate, citrate, classmate, cognate, collate, comate, connate, cordate, costate, create, cremate, crenate, crispate, cristate, curate, curvate, debate, deflate, delate, dentate, dictate, dilate, donate, elate, equate, estate, falcate, filtrate, flyweight, formate, frontate, frustrate, furcate, gemmate, globate, gradate, guttate, gyrate, hamate, hastate, helpmate, hydrate, inflate, ingrate, inmate, innate, instate, irate, jugate, khanate, Kuwait, lactate, larvate, legate, lichgate, ligate, lightweight, lobate, locate, lunate, lustrate, magnate, mandate, messmate, migrate, misdate, mismate, misstate, mutate, narrate, negate, nervate, nictate, nitrate, notate, nutate, oblate, orate, ornate, ovate, palate, palmate, palpate, peltate, pennate, phonate, phosphate, picrate, pinnate, placate, playmate, prelate, primate, private, probate, prolate, prorate, prostate, prostrate, pulsate, punctuate, quadrate, quinate, rebate, relate, restate, rotate, rugate, sedate, septate, serrate, shipmate, sigmate, spicate, stagnate, stalemate, stannate, stellate, striate, sublate, sulcate, sulfate, tannate, tartrate, template, ternate, testate, titrate, tractate, translate, truncate, vacate, vibrate, Vulgate, xanthate, zonate; abdicate, ablactate, abnegate, abrogate, accurate, acetate, actuate, addlepate, adequate, adulate, adumbrate, advocate, aggravate, aggregate, agitate, allocate, altercate, alternate, ambulate, amputate, animate, annotate, annulate, antedate, antiquate, apostate, appellate, approbate, arbitrate, arrogate, aspirate, aureate, aviate, bifurcate, Billingsgate, brachiate, bracteate, branchiate, cachinnate, calculate, calibrate, caliphate, cancellate, candidate, captivate, carbonate, castigate, catenate, celibate, cellulate, chloridate, ciliate, circulate, clypeate, cochleate, cogitate, colligate, collimate, collocate, comminate, compensate, complicate, concentrate, confiscate, conformate, conglobate, congregate, conjugate, consecrate, constipate, consulate, consummate, contemplate, copulate, cornuate, coronate, corporate, correlate, corrugate, corticate, coruscate, crenellate, crenulate, crepitate, cucullate, culminate, cultivate, cumulate, cuneate, cuspidate, cyanate, decimate, declinate, decollate, decorate, decussate, dedicate, defalcate, defecate, dehydrate, delegate, delicate, demarcate, demonstrate, denigrate, denudate, depilate, deprecate, depredate, derogate, desecrate, desiccate, designate, desolate, desperate, detonate, devastate, deviate, digitate, diplomate, dislocate, disparate, dissipate, distillate, divagate, doctorate, dominate, duplicate, ebriate, echinate, edentate, educate, elevate, elongate, emanate, emigrate, emulate, enervate, eructate, estimate, estivate, excavate, exculpate, execrate, expiate, explanate, explicate, expurgate, extirpate, extricate, fabricate, fascinate, featherweight, fecundate, federate, fenestrate, fibrillate, fistulate, flagellate, floriate, fluctuate, fluorate, foliate, formicate, formulate, fornicate, fortunate, fructuate, fulgurate, fulminate, fumigate, geminate, generate, germinate, glaciate, gladiate, glomerate, Golden Gate, graduate, granulate, gravitate, heavyweight, hebetate, hesitate, hibernate, hyphenate, ideate, illustrate, imbricate, imitate, immigrate, immolate, implicate, imprecate, impregnate, improvisate, incarnate, inchoate, incrassate, incubate, inculcate, inculpate, incurvate, indicate, indurate, infiltrate, innervate, innovate, inornate, insensate, insolate, inspissate, instigate, insufflate, insulate, integrate, interstate, intestate, intimate, intonate, intricate, inundate, irrigate, irritate,

isolate, iterate, jubilate, labiate, lacerate,
lamellate, laminate, lancinate, lapidate,
laureate, legislate, levirate, levitate, liber-
ate, ligulate, lineate, liquidate, literate, liti-
gate, loricate, lubricate, lucubrate, macer-
ate, machinate, maculate, magistrate,
majorate, manducate, manganate, margin-
ate, margravate, marquisate, masticate,
maturate, mediate, medicate, meditate,
menstruate, methylate, micturate, militate,
mitigate, moderate, modulate, molybdate,
motivate, muriate, mutilate, nauseate, nav-
igate, nictitate, niobate, nominate, nucle-
ate, obfuscate, objurgate, obligate, obo-
vate, obstinate, obviate, oculate, oleate,
omoplate, opiate, orchestrate, ordinate, os-
cillate, oscitate, osculate, overrate, over-
state, overweight, ovulate, paginate, palli-
ate, palpitate, paperweight, papillate,
passionate, pastorate, patellate, pectinate,
peculate, pejorate, pendulate, penetrate,
percolate, perforate, permeate, perorate,
perpetrate, personate, phosphorate, pileate,
pollinate, populate, postulate, potentate,
predicate, principate, priorate, procreate,
profligate, promulgate, propagate, propin-
quate, proximate, prussiate, pullulate, pul-
monate, pulverate, pulvinate, punctuate,
punctulate, pustulate, radiate, radicate, rec-
linate, recreate, rectorate, recurvate, regu-
late, reinstate, relegate, remigrate, remon-
strate, renovate, replicate, reprobate,
resonate, roseate, rostellate, rubricate, ru-
minate, rusticate, sagittate, salivate, sani-
tate, satiate, saturate, scintillate, scutellate,
segmentate, segregate, selenate, separate,

septenate, sequestrate, seriate, serrulate, shogunate, sibilate, silicate, simulate, sinuate, situate, spatulate, speculate, spiculate, spiflicate, spoliate, staminate, stearate, stellulate, stimulate, stipulate, strangulate, stylobate, subjugate, sublimate, subulate, suffocate, sulfurate, sultanate, supinate, supplicate, suppurate, surrogate, syncopate, syndicate, tabulate, tellurate, temperate, titanate, titillate, titivate, tolerate, toluate, trabeate, tracheate, transmigrate, tridentate, trijugate, trilobate, triplicate, trisulcate, triturate, tubulate, tunicate, turbinate, ulcerate, ultimate, ululate, umbellate, uncinate, undulate, underrate, understate, underweight, ungulate, urinate, urticate, ustulate, vaccinate, vacillate, vaginate, valerate, validate, vanillate, variate, vegetate, venerate, ventilate, vertebrate, vesicate, vindicate, violate, viscerate, vitiate, Watergate, welterweight; abbreviate, abominate, accelerate, accentuate, accommodate, accumulate, acidulate, acuminate, adjudicate, adulterate, affectionate, affiliate, agglomerate, agglutinate, aldermanate, alienate, alleviate, amalgamate, annihilate, annunciate, anticipate, apiculate, apostolate, appreciate, appropinquate, appropriate, approximate, areolate, articulate, asphyxiate, assassinate, asseverate, assimilate, associate, attenuate, auriculate, authenticate, calumniate, capitulate, centuplicate, certificate, chalybeate, circumvallate, coagulate, coelenterate, collaborate, collegiate, commemorate, commensurate, commiserate, communicate, compassionate, concatenate, conciliate, confabulate, confederate, conglomerate, conglutinate, congratulate, considerate, consolidate, contaminate, conterminate, continuate, cooperate, coordinate, corroborate, corymbiate, curvicaudate, curvicostate, debilitate, decapitate, decemvirate, degenerate, deglutinate, deliberate, delineate, denominate, denticulate, denunciate, depopulate, depreciate, deracinate, desiderate, determinate, debranchiate, dictatorate, dilapidate, directorate, disconsolate, discriminate, dispassionate, disseminate, dissimulate, dissociate, divaricate, domesticate, duumvirate, ebracteate, effectuate, effeminate, ejaculate, elaborate, electorate, electroplate, eliminate, elucidate, emaciate, emancipate, emasculate, enucleate, enumerate, enunciate, episcopate, equilibrate, equivocate, eradiate, eradicate, etiolate, evacuate, evaginate, evaluate, evaporate, eventuate, eviscerate, exacerbate, exaggerate, examinate, exasperate, excogitate, excoriate, excruciate, exfoliate, exhilarate, exonerate, expatiate, expatriate, expectorate, expostulate, expropriate, exsanguinate, extenuate, exterminate, extortionate, extrapolate, extravagate, exuberate, facilitate, felicitate, foraminate, gelatinate, geniculate, gesticulate, habilitate, habituate, hallucinate, horripilate, humiliate, hydrogenate, hypothecate, illiterate, illuminate, immaculate, immediate, immoderate, imperforate, impersonate, importunate, impostumate, impropriate, inaccurate, inadequate, inanimate, inaugurate, incarcerate, incinerate, incorporate, incriminate, indelicate, indoctrinate, inebriate, infatuate, infuriate, ingeminate, ingratiate, ingurgitate, initiate, innominate, inoculate, inordinate, insatiate, inseminate, inseparate, insinuate, inspectorate, intemperate, intercalate, interminate, interpolate, interrogate, intimidate, intoxicate, invaginate, invalidate, invertebrate, investigate, inveterate, invigorate, inviolate, irradiate, irradicate, itinerate, lanceolate, legitimate, licentiate, lineolate, lixiviate, luxuriate, machicolate, mandibulate, manipulate, marsupiate, matriarchate, matriculate, meliorate, miscalculate, multidentate, multilobate, multiplicate, necessitate, negotiate, nidificate, novitiate, nudirostrate, obliterate, officiate, operate, operculate, orbiculate, orientate, originate, oxygenate, pacificate, palatinate, paniculate, participate, particulate, patriarchate, pediculate, penultimate, peregrinate, permanganate, perpetuate, petiolate, pomegranate, pontificate, postgraduate, precipitate, precogitate, preconsulate, predestinate, predominate, prejudicate, premeditate, prenominate, prevaricate, procrastinate, prognosticate, proliferate, propitiate, proportionate, protectorate, protuberate, quadruplicate, quintuplicate, reanimate, recalcitrate, reciprocate, recriminate, recuperate, redecorate, reduplicate, refrigerate, regenerate, regurgitate, reiterate, rejuvenate, remunerate, repatriate, repopulate, repudiate, resuscitate, retaliate, reticulate, reverberate, salicylate, somnambulate, sophisticate, subordinate, substanti-

ate, syllabicate, tergiversate, testiculate,
testudinate, trabeculate, transliterate, trian-
gulate, tricorporate, trifoliate, triumvirate,
variegate, vermiculate, vesiculate, vestibu-
late, vicariate, vituperate, vociferate; amel-
iorate, baccalaureate, canaliculate, circum-
ambulate, circumnavigate, circumstantiate,
consubstantiate, deoxygenate, deteriorate,
differentiate, discombobulate, dispropor-
tionate, domiciliate, excommunicate, imbe-
cilitate, incapacitate, intermediate, latifoli-
ate, misappropriate, predeterminate,
proletariat, quadrifoliate, quadrigeminate,
quinquefoliate, ratiocinate, recapitulate, re-
habilitate, reinvigorate, secretariate, super-
annuate, supererogate, transubstantiate,
trifoliolate, undergraduate, unifoliate.

-ath (-ath), bath, Bath, Gath, hath, lath,
math, path, rath, snath, wrath; birdbath,
bloodbath, bypath, towpath, warpath; af-
termath, allopath, psychopath; homeopath,
osteopath.

-ath (-ôth). See **-oth.**

-athe, bathe, lathe, scathe, swathe; un-
swathe.

-au (-ou). See **-ow** (-ou).

-au (-ō). See **-ow** (-ō).

-auce. See **-oss.**

-aud, bawd, broad, Claude, fraud, gaud,
laud, Maud; abroad, applaud, belaud, de-
fraud, maraud.

    Also: **-aw** + **-ed** (as in *clawed,* etc.)

-augh. See **-aff.**

-aught. See **-ought** or **-aft.**

-aul. See **-awl.**

-auled. See **-ald.**

-ault. See **-alt.**

-aunch, craunch, haunch, launch, paunch, staunch.

-aunt, aunt, daunt, flaunt, gaunt, haunt, jaunt, taunt, vaunt, want; avaunt, keeshond, romaunt; bon vivant, confidant, debutante, dilettante, restaurant.

-aunts. See **-ounce.**

-ause, cause, clause, gauze, hawse, pause, yaws; applause, because; menopause, Santa Claus.

    Also: **-aw** + **-s** (as in *claws*, etc.)

-aust. See **-ost.**

-aut. See **-ot** and **-ought.**

-ave (-av). See **-alve.**

-ave (-āv), brave, cave, crave, Dave, gave, glaive, grave, knave, lave, nave, pave, rave, save, shave, slave, stave, suave, they've, waive, wave; behave, concave, conclave, deprave, enclave, engrave, enslave, exclave, forgave, margrave, misgave, octave; architrave, microwave.

-aw, awe, caw, chaw, claw, craw, daw, draw, faugh, flaw, gnaw, haw, jaw, law, maw, paw, pshaw, raw, saw, Shaw, squaw, straw, taw, thaw, yaw; catspaw, coleslaw, cushaw, foresaw, gewgaw, guffaw, heehaw, jackdaw, jigsaw, macaw, papaw, seesaw, southpaw, Warsaw, withdraw; Arkansas, mackinaw, Omaha, Ottawa, overawe, Panama.

-awd. See **-aud.**

-awed. See **-aud.**

-awk. See **-alk.**

-awl, all, awl, ball, bawl, brawl, call, crawl,
drawl, fall, gall, Gaul, hall, haul, mall,
maul, pall, Paul, pawl, Saul, scrawl,
shawl, small, sprawl, squall, stall, tall,
thrall, trawl, wall, y'all, yawl; Algol,
ALGOL, appall, AWOL, baseball, befall,
Bengal, catcall, COBOL, cure-all, curveball,
enthrall, football, footfall, forestall, googol,
install, rainfall, recall, shortfall, snowfall,
Whitehall, windfall; aerosol, alcohol, bas-
ketball, cannonball, caterwaul, free-for-all,
gasohol, overhaul, pentothal, volleyball,
waterfall, wherewithal; cholesterol, Nean-
derthal.

-awled. See **-ald.**

-awn. See **-on** (ôn).

-aws. See **-ause.**

-ax, ax, fax, flax, lax, Max, pax, sax, tax,
wax; addax, Ajax, anthrax, climax, relax,
syntax, thorax; battleax, Halifax, Kallikaks,
parallax; Adirondacks, anticlimax, Astya-
nax.

Also: **-ack** + **-s** (as in *sacks,* etc.)

-ay, (-ā), a, aye, bay, bey, brae, bray, clay,
day, dray, ey, fay, Fay, fey, flay, fray, gay,
gray, grey, hay, jay, Kay, lay, Mae, may,
May, nay, née, neigh, pay, play, pray,
prey, ray, Ray, say, shay, slay, sleigh,
spay, spray, stay, stray, sway, they, trait,
tray, trey, way, weigh, whey; abbé, affray,
agley, allay, array, assay, astray, away,
ballet, belay, beret, betray, bewray, Bom-
bay, bomb bay, bouquet, Broadway, café,
Calais, Cathay, causeway, chambray, con-
vey, coupé, Courbet, croquet, curé, decay,

defray, delay, dengue, dismay, display, distrait, doomsday, dragée, endplay, essay, filet, fillet, foray, foreplay, Fouquet, foyer, Friday, gainsay, gangway, hearsay, heyday, horseplay, inlay, inveigh, Koine, Malay, Manet, May Day, melee, midday, mislay, moiré, Monday, Monet, moray, nosegay, obey, okay, ole!, passé, per se, pince-nez, portray, prepay, purée, purvey, Rabelais, relay, repay, risqué, Roget, roué, sachet, sashay, soirée, soufflé, subway, Sunday, survey, throughway, Thursday, today, tokay, touché, toupée, Tuesday, veejay, waylay, Wednesday; appliqué, bad hair day, Beaujolais, cabaret, canapé, castaway, Chevrolet, consommé, deMusset, disarray, disobey, distingué, DNA, émigré, exposé, faraway, fiancé(e), holiday, Mandalay, matinee, Milky Way, Monterey, Monterrey, negligée, Nez Percé, Plug and Play, popinjay, protégé(e), résumé, roundelay, runaway, Saint-Tropez, Salomé, Santa Fe, Saturday, s'il vous plaît, sobriquet, stowaway, Tenebrae, virelay, yesterday; Appian Way, bichon frisé, cabriolet, café au lait, caloo-calay, communiqué, Dies Irae, felo-de-se, habitué, Olivier, papier-maché, roman à clef, sine die, sotto voce, sub judice; arrière pensée, Mrs. Dalloway; cinema verité; Edna St. Vincent Millay.

-ayed. See **-ade.**

-ays. See **-aze.**

-aze, baize, blaze, braise, braze, chaise, craze, daze, faze, gaze, glaze, graze, haze, maize, maze, phase, phrase, praise, raise, raze; ablaze, amaze, appraise, catchphrase, dispraise, liaise, malaise, stargaze, ukase; chrysoprase, lyonnaise, Marseillaise, mayonnaise, nowadays, overgraze, paraphrase, polonaise, underglaze.

   Also: **-ay** + **-s** (as in *days*, etc.)
   Also: **-ey** + **-s** (as in *preys*, etc.)
   Also: **-eigh** + **-s** (as in *weighs*, etc.)

-azz, as, has, jazz, razz; pizzazz, topaz, whereas; Alcatraz, razzmatazz.

-e. See **-ee.**

-ea. See **-ee.**

-eace. See **-ease.**

-each, beach, beech, bleach, breach, breech, each, leach, leech, peach, preach, reach, screech, speech, teach; beseech, impeach; overreach.

-ead (-ēd). See **-eed.**

-ead (-ed). See **-ed.**

-eaf (-ef). See **-ef.**

-eaf (-ēf). See **-ief.**

-eague, gigue, Grieg, klieg, league; blitzkrieg, colleague, enleague, fatigue, intrigue.

-eak (-ēk), beak, bleak, cheek, chic, clique, creak, creek, eke, freak, geek, Greek, leak, leek, meek, peak, peek, pique, reek, seek, sheik, shriek, Sikh, sleek, sneak, speak, squeak, streak, teak, tweak, weak, week, wreak; antique, Belleek, bespeak, bezique, cacique, critique, Monique, mystique, oblique, physique, relique, unique; Chesapeake, fenugreek, Frederique, Martinique, Mozambique, Pathétique.

-eak (-āk). See **-ake.**

-eal, ceil, creel, deal, eel, feel, heal, heel, he'll, keel, Kiel, kneel, leal, meal, Neal, Neil, peal, peel, real, reel, seal, she'll, spiel, squeal, steal, teal, veal, weal, we'll, wheel, zeal; anele, anneal, appeal, Bastille, cartwheel, Castile, chenille, conceal, congeal, cornmeal, Émile, fourwheel, genteel, ideal, Lucille, misdeal, mobile, Mobile, oatmeal, pastille, repeal, reveal, Tarheel, unreal; camomile, campanile, cochineal, commonweal, deshabille, difficile, glockenspiel, mercantile, snowmobile; automobile.

-eald. See **-ield.**

-ealed. See **-ield.**

-ealm. See **-elm.**

-ealth, health, stealth, wealth; commonwealth.

-eam, beam, bream, cream, deem, dream, fleam, gleam, ream, scheme, scream, seam, seem, steam, stream, team, teem, theme; abeam, beseem, blaspheme, bloodstream, centime, daydream, dream team, esteem, extreme, ice cream, moonbeam, redeem, regime, supreme, trireme; academe, self-esteem; ancien régime.

-ean, bean, been, clean, dean, Dean, e'en, Gene, glean, green, Jean, keen, lean, lien, mean, mien, peen, preen, quean, queen, scene, screen, seen, sheen, spleen, teen, wean, ween, yean; baleen, beguine, benzine, between, caffeine, canteen, careen, chlorine, Christine, codeine, colleen, convene, cuisine, demean, demesne, eighteen, Eileen, Eugene, fifteen, foreseen, fourteen, ich dien, Kathleen, machine, marine, nine-

teen, obscene, Pauline, poteen, praline,
protein, quinine, ravine, routine, sardine,
serene, shagreen, sixteen, subvene, thir-
teen, tontine, tureen, unclean; Aberdeen,
Abilene, Argentine, atabrine, atropine,
barkentine, Benzedrine, bombazine, brig-
antine, contravene, crêpe de chine, dama-
scene, evergreen, fellahin, Florentine, gab-
ardine, gasoline, Geraldine, Ghibelline,
guillotine, intervene, Josephine, kerosene,
libertine, magazine, mezzanine, mousse-
line, Nazarene, nectarine, nicotine, over-
seen, Paris green, Philistine, quarantine,
serpentine, seventeen, submarine, tambou-
rine, tangerine, unforeseen, Vaseline, vel-
veteen, wolverine; acetylene, alexandrine,
amphetamine, aquamarine, Benedictine, elephantine, incarnadine, nouvelle cuisine,
ultramarine.

-eaned. See **-iend.**

-eant. See **-ent.**

-eap. See **-eep.**

-ear. See **-eer.**

-earch. See **-urch.**

-eard (-ird), beard, tiered, weird; afeard,
dog-eared.
    Also: **-ear** + **-ed** (as in *reared*, etc.)
    Also: **-ere** + **-ed** (as in *interfered*, etc.)
    Also: **-eer** + **-ed** (as in *veered*, etc.)

-eard (-ûrd). See **-urd.**

-eared. See **-eard.**

-earl. See **-url.**

-earn. See **-urn.**

-ears. See **-ares.**

-earse. See **-erse.**

-eart. See **-art.**

-earth. See **-irth.**

-eas. See **-ease.**

-ease (-ēs), cease, crease, fleece, geese, grease, Greece, lease, Nice, niece, peace, piece; Bernice, caprice, decease, decrease, increase, Maurice, obese, pelisse, police, release, surcease, valise; altarpiece, ambergris, diocese, frontispiece, mantelpiece, masterpiece, predecease, Singalese.

-ease (-ēz), bise, breeze, cheese, ease, freeze, frieze, grease, he's, lees, pease, please, seize, she's, skis, sneeze, squeeze, tease, these, wheeze; appease, Burmese, cerise, chemise, Chinese, disease, displease, Louise, Maltese, Pisces, Thales, trapeze; ABC's, Achilles, Androcles, antifreeze, Antilles, Balinese, Brooklynese, Cantonese, Damocles, Heloise, Hercules, Japanese, Javanese, journalese, legalese, obsequies, overseas, Pekinese, Pleiades, Portuguese, Siamese, Viennese; anopheles, antipodes, antitheses, computerese, Hippocrates, hypotheses, parentheses, Peloponnese, soliloquies, Vietnamese; aborigines, Mephistopheles.

  Also: **-ea** + **-s** (as in *teas*, etc.)

  Also: **-ee** + **-s** (as in *bees*, *frees*, etc.)

-eased. See **-east.**

-east, beast, east, feast, least, priest, yeast; artiste.

  Also: **-ease** + **-ed** (as in *released*, etc.)

-eat (-ēt), beat, beet, bleat, cheat, Crete, eat, feat, feet, fleet, greet, heat, meat, meet, mete, neat, peat, Pete, pleat, seat, sheet,

skeet, sleet, street, suite, sweet, teat, treat,
wheat; accrete, aesthete, afreet, athlete,
backstreet, compete, complete, conceit,
concrete, deadbeat, deceit, defeat, delete,
deplete, discreet, discrete, effete, elite, en-
treat, mainsheet, petite, receipt, replete, re-
treat, secrete; bittersweet, Easy Street, in-
complete, indiscreet, Marguerite, obsolete,
overeat, parakeet.

-eat (-āt). See **-ate.**

-eat (-et). See **-et.**

-eath (-eth), Beth, breath, death, saith, Seth;
Macbeth; Ashtoreth; shibboleth; Elizabeth.

-eath (-ēth), heath, Keith, 'neath, sheath,
teeth, wreath; beneath; underneath.

-eathe (-ēth), breathe, seethe, sheathe,
teethe, wreathe; bequeath, enwreathe.

-eau. See **-ow.**

-eave (-ēv), breve, cleave, eave, eve, Eve,
grieve, heave, leave, lieve, peeve, reave,
reeve, sleeve, Steve, thieve, weave, we've;
achieve, aggrieve, believe, bereave, con-
ceive, deceive, khedive, naïve, perceive,
qui vive, receive, relieve, reprieve, re-
trieve; disbelieve, Genevieve, interleave,
make-believe, Tel Aviv; overachieve, reci-
tative, underachieve.

-eb, bleb, deb, ebb, neb, reb, web; World
Wide Web.

-eck, beck, check, cheque, Czech, deck,
fleck, heck, neck, peck, reck, speck, tech,
trek, wreck; bedeck, henpeck, Quebec, Star
Trek; à la greque, bottleneck, demi-sec,
discotheque, rubberneck, turtleneck; Te-
huantepec.

-ecked. See **-ect.**

-ecks. See **-ex.**

-ect, sect; abject, affect, bisect, collect, con-
nect, correct, defect, deflect, deject, detect,
direct, dissect, effect, eject, elect, erect, ex-
pect, infect, inject, inspect, neglect, object,
pandect, perfect, prefect, project, prospect,
protect, reflect, reject, respect, select, sub-
ject, suspect; architect, circumspect, dia-
lect, disconnect, disrespect, incorrect, intel-
lect, interject, intersect, introspect,
misdirect, recollect, retrospect, vivisect.
    Also: **-eck** + **-ed** (as in *wrecked,* etc.)

-ed, bed, bled, bread, bred, dead, dread, Ed,
fed, fled, Fred, head, Jed, lead, led, Ned,
pled, read, red, said, shed, shred, sled,
sped, spread, stead, ted, Ted, thread,
tread, wed, zed; abed, ahead, airhead,
beachhead, behead, biped, Club Med,
coed, crossbred, deadhead, death's-head,
egghead, forehead, godhead, hogshead, in-
bred, instead, misled, moped, Op-Ed, out-
spread, unread, unsaid; aforesaid, foun-
tainhead, gingerbread, hammerhead,
letterhead, loggerhead, maidenhead, quad-
ruped, sleepyhead, thoroughbred, under-
fed, watershed.

-ede. See **-eed.**

-edge, dredge, edge, fledge, hedge, kedge,
ledge, pledge, sedge, sledge, wedge; allege,
unedge.

-ee, be, Bea, bee, Brie, Cree, fee, flea, flee,
free, gee, glee, he, key, knee, lea, lee, me,
pea, plea, quay, sea, see, she, ski, spree,
tea, thee, three, tree, we, wee, ye; acme,

acne, agree, bohea, CD, Darcy, debris, decree, degree, Dundee, ennui, foresee, goatee, grandee, grantee, lessee, levee, Marie, marquee, marquis, Mowgli, Parsee, rupee, settee, spondee, trochee, trustee; ABC, abscissae, absentee, adobe, addressee, agony, alumnae, anomie, amputee, apogee, assignee, baloney, botany, bourgeoisie, bumblebee, calorie, calumny, canopy, Cherokee, chickadee, chimpanzee, C.O.D., company, coterie, DDT, debauchee, destiny, devotee, disagree, ebony, felony, filagree, fleur-de-lis, fricassee, gelati, gluttony, guarantee, harmony, irony, jamboree, licensee, Lombardy, Maccabee, maître d', manatee, nepenthe, Niobe, nominee, Normandy, pedigree, perigee, Pharisee, Picardy, potpourri, Ptolemy, recipe, referee, refugee, repartee, reveille, Sadducee, satori, sesame, symphony, syzygy, tyranny, VIP, vis-à-vis, wannabe; abalone, anemone, anomaly, apostrophe, Antigone, Ariadne, bouquet garni, caller ID, calliope, catastrophe, digerati, Euphrosyne, facsimile, fait accompli, Gethsemane, hyperbole, Karaoke, macaroni, Melpomene, Penelope, proclivity, synonymy; aborigine, Deuteronomy.

-eece. See **-ease.**

-eech. See **-each.**

-eed, bead, Bede, bleed, breed, cede, creed, deed, feed, freed, greed, heed, keyed, knead, lead, mead, Mede, meed, need, plead, read, reed, seed, screed, speed, steed, Swede, tweed, weed; Candide, concede, decreed, exceed, Godspeed, impede,

indeed, misdeed, mislead, precede, pro-
ceed, recede, secede, stampede, succeed;
aniseed, antecede, centipede, Ganymede,
intercede, ironweed, millipede, overfeed,
Runnymede, supersede; velocipede; Nie-
belungenlied.

Also: **-ee** + **-ed** (as in *agreed,* etc.)

-eef. See **-ief.**

-eek. See **-eak.**

-eel. See **-eal.**

-eeled. See **-ield.**

-eem. See **-eam.**

-een. See **-ean.**

-eened. See **-iend.**

-eep, cheap, cheep, creep, deep, heap, jeep,
keep, leap, neap, peep, reap, seep, sheep,
sleep, steep, sweep, veep, weep; asleep,
beweep, upkeep; oversleep; Uriah Heep.

-eer, beer, bier, blear, cheer, clear, dear,
deer, drear, ear, fear, fleer, gear, hear,
here, jeer, Lear, leer, mere, near, peer,
pier, queer, rear, schmear, sear, seer, sere,
shear, sheer, smear, sneer, spear, sphere,
steer, tear, tier, veer, weir, year; adhere,
amir, ampere, appear, arrear, austere,
brassière, career, cashier, cashmere, co-
here, compeer, emir, endear, frontier, in-
here, reindeer, revere, severe, sincere, Tan-
gier, veneer; atmosphere, auctioneer,
bandoleer, bombardier, brigadier, bucca-
neer, cannoneer, cavalier, chandelier,
chanticleer, chiffonier, commandeer, disap-
pear, domineer, engineer, financier, frontier, gazeteer, gondolier, grenadier, Guine-
vere, hemisphere, insincere, interfere,

jardiniere, mountaineer, muleteer, musketeer, mutineer, overhear, overseer, pamphleteer, persevere, pioneer, privateer, profiteer, souvenir, volunteer; charioteer, electioneer.

-eered. See **-eard.**

-ees. See **-ease** (-ēz).

-eese. See **-ease** (-ēs).

-eet. See **-eat.**

-eethe. See **-eathe.**

-eeze. See **-ease.**

-ef, chef, clef, deaf, Jeff; aleph, tone-deaf.

-eft, cleft, deft, eft, heft, left, reft, theft, weft; bereft.

-eg, beg, dreg, egg, keg, leg, Meg, peg, Peg, skeg, yegg; nutmeg, pegleg, renege; philibeg, Winnipeg.

-ege (-ezh), barege, cortege, manège.

-ege (-ij). See **-age.**

-egm. See **-em.**

-eigh. See **-ay.**

-eighed. See **-ade.**

-eighs. See **-aze.**

-eight (-āt). See **-ate.**

-eight (-īt). See **-ite.**

-eign. See **-ain.**

-eil (-āl). See **-ail.**

-eil (-ēl). See **-eal.**

-ein (-ān). See **-ain.**

-ein (-īn). See **-ine.**

-eint. See **-aint.**

-eir. See **-are.**

-eird. See **-eard.**

-eirs. See **-ares.**

-eive. See **-eave.**

-eize. See **-ease.**

-eke. See **-eak.**

-el, bell, belle, Belle, cell, dell, dwell, ell, fell, hell, jell, knell, Nell, quell, sell, shell, smell, spell, swell, tell, well, yell; appel, befell, Boswell, compel, Cornell, dispel, Estelle, excel, expel, foretell, gazelle, hotel, impel, lapel, Moselle, pastel, pell-mell, prequel, rebel, repel, sequel; asphodel, Astrophel, bagatelle, calomel, caravel, caromel, Chanterelle, citadel, clientele, decibel, hydromel, infidel, Jezebel, muscatel, parallel, personnel, philomel, pimpernel, sentinel, undersell, villanelle, zinfandel; mademoiselle.

-elch, belch, squelch.

-eld, eld, geld, held, weld; beheld, unquelled, upheld, withheld.

Also: **-ell** + **-ed** (as in *spelled*, etc.)

-elf, delf, elf, Guelph, pelf, self, shelf; herself, himself, itself, myself, ourself, thyself, yourself.

-elk, elk, whelk.

-ell. See **-el.**

-elle. See **-el.**

-elled. See **-eld.**

-elm, elm, helm, realm, whelm; overwhelm, underwhelm.

-elp, help, kelp, whelp, yelp; self-help.

-elt, belt, Celt, dealt, dwelt, felt, Kelt, knelt, melt, pelt, smelt, spelt, svelte, veldt, welt; black belt, greenbelt, snowbelt, Sunbelt.

-elve, delve, helve, shelve, twelve.

-em, crème, em, femme, gem, hem, phlegm,

REM, Shem, stem; them; adquem, ad rem, ahem, begem, condemn, contemn, modem, pro tem; apothegm, ATM, Bethlehem, diadem, requiem, strategem, theorem; ad hominem.

-eme. See **-eam.**

-emn. See **-em.**

-empt, dreamt, kempt, tempt; attempt, contempt, exempt, pre-empt, unkempt; taxexempt.

-en, Ben, den, fen, glen, Gwen, hen, ken, men, pen, Seine, ten, then, wen, when, wren, yen, Zen; again, amen, Cheyenne; allergen, citizen, hydrogen, julienne, mise en scène, nitrogen, oxygen, Saracen, specimen; carcinogen, comedienne, equestrienne, Parisienne, tragedienne.

-ence, cense, dense, fence, hence, pence, sense, tense, thence, whence; commence, condense, defense, dispense, expense, Hortense, immense, incense, intense, offense, pretense, suspense; abstinence, accidence, affluence, ambience, audience, confidence, consequence, continence, difference, diffidence, diligence, eloquence, eminence, evidence, excellence, frankincense, immanence, imminence, impotence, impudence, indigence, indolence, inference, influence, innocence, negligence, opulence, penitence, preference, providence, recompense, redolence, reference, residence, reticence, reverence, sapience, truculence, turbulence, vehemence, violence, virulence; beneficence, benevolence, circumference, grandiloquence, inconsequence, intelligence, intransigence, magnificence, munificence, obedience, omnipotence, preeminence, subservience.

Also: **-ent** + **-s** (as in *tents*, etc.)

-enced. See **-ainst**.

-ench, bench, blench, clench, drench, flench, French, mensch, quench, stench, tench, trench, wench, wrench; intrench, retrench.

-end, bend, blend, end, fend, friend, lend, mend, rend, send, spend, tend, trend, vend, wend; amend, append, ascend, attend, befriend, commend, contend, dead end, defend, depend, descend, distend, emend, expend, extend, forefend, impend, intend, misspend, offend, pitchblende, portend, pretend, stipend, suspend, transcend, unbend, weekend; apprehend, comprehend, condescend, dividend, minuend, recommend, reprehend, subtrahend; misapprehend, overextend, superintend.

Also: **-en** + **-ed** (as in *penned*, etc.)

-ene. See **-ean**.

-enge, avenge, revenge; Stonehenge.

-ength, length, strength; full-length.

-enned. See **-end**.

-ens. See **-ense**.

-ense (-enz). See **-ence**.

-ense (-enz), cleanse, gens, lens.

Also: **-en** + **-s** (as in *pens*, etc.)

Also: **-end** + **-s** (as in *bends*, etc.)

-ensed. See **-ainst**.

-ent, bent, blent, cent, dent, gent, Ghent, Kent, leant, lent, Lent, meant, pent, rent, scent, sent, spent, tent, Trent, vent, went; absent, accent, anent, ascent, assent, augment, cement, comment, consent, content, descent, detent, dissent, event, extent, ferment, foment, frequent, indent, intent, invent, lament, misspent, portent, present, prevent, relent, repent, resent, torment, unbent, unspent; abstinent, accident, aliment, argument, armament, banishment, battlement, betterment, blandishment, chastisement, competent, complement, compliment, condiment, confident, consequent, continent, detriment, different, diffident, diligent, dissident, document, element, eloquent, eminent, evident, excellent, exigent, filament, firmament, fraudulent, government, immanent, imminent, implement, impotent, impudent, incident, increment, indigent, innocent, insolent, instrument, languishment, liniment, malcontent, management, measurement, merriment, monument, negligent, nourishment, nutriment, occident, opulent, orient, ornament, overspent, parliament, penitent, permanent, pertinent, precedent, president, prevalent, provident, punishment, ravishment, redolent, regiment, represent, resident, reticent, reverent, rudiment, sacrament, sentiment, settlement, subsequent, succulent, supplement, temperament, tenement, testament, underwent, vehement, violent, virulent, wonderment; accomplishment, acknowledgment, advertisement, astonishment, belligerent, benevolent, development, disarmament, embarrassment, embodiment, enlightenment, environment, establishment, experiment, impenitent, impertinent, imprisonment, improvident, intelligent, irreverent, magnificent, magniloquent, presentiment, subservient, temperament; accompaniment.

-ep, hep, nep, pep, prep, rep, repp, step, steppe, yep; Dieppe, footstep, lockstep, misstep, sidestep; Amenhotep.

-ept, drept, kept, sept, slept, stepped, swept, wept; accept, adept, except, inept, precept, windswept, yclept; intercept, overslept.

er, blur, bur, burr, cur, err, fir, fur, her, myrrh, per, purr, shirr, sir, slur, spur, stir, were, whir; astir, aver, Ben Hur, bestir, Big Sur, chasseur, chauffeur, coiffeur, concur, confer, defer, demur, deter, hauteur, incur, infer, inter, jongleur, larkspur, liqueur, occur, prefer, recur, refer, seigneur, transfer; amateur, arbiter, barrister, calendar, chronicler, chorister, colander, comforter, connoisseur, cri de coeur, cylinder, de rigueur, disinter, dowager, gossamer, harbinger, Jennifer, Jupiter, lavender, Lucifer, mariner, massacre, messenger, minister, officer, passenger, prisoner, raconteur, register, scimitar, sepulcher, traveler, voyageur; administer, astrologer, astronomer, barometer, entrepreneur, Excalibur, idolater, restaurateur, thermometer.

-erb, blurb, curb, herb, kerb, Serb, verb; acerb, adverb, disturb, perturb, suburb, superb.

-erce. See **-erse.**

-erced. See **-urst.**

-erch. See **-urch.**

-erd. See **-urd.**

-ere (-ār). See **-are.**

-ere (-ēr). See **-eer.**

-ered. See **-eard.**

-erf. See **-urf.**

-erg, berg, burgh; iceberg.

-erge, dirge, merge, purge, scourge, serge, splurge, spurge, surge, urge, verge; absterge, converge, deterge, diverge, emerge, immerge, submerge; demiurge, dramaturge, thaumaturge.

-erm. See **-irm.**

-ern. See **-urn.**

-err. See **-er.**

-erred. See **-urd.**

-erse, curse, Erse, hearse, herse, nurse, purse, terse, verse, worse; accurse, adverse, amerce, asperse, averse, coerce, commerce, converse, disburse, disperse, diverse, imburse, immerse, inverse, obverse, perverse, rehearse, reverse, traverse, transverse; intersperse, reimburse, universe.

-ersed. See **-urst.**

-ert, Bert, blurt, Burt, curt, dirt, flirt, Gert, girt, hurt, Kurt, pert, shirt, skirt, spurt, squirt, wert, wort; advert, Albert, alert, assert, avert, concert, convert, covert, desert, dessert, divert, evert, exert, expert, filbert, Herbert, inert, insert, invert, overt, pervert, revert, subvert, T-shirt, unhurt; controvert, disconcert, extrovert, introvert; animadvert.

-erth. See **-irth.**

-erve, curve, Irv, nerve, serve, swerve, verve; conserve, deserve, hors d'oeuvre,

incurve, innerve, observe, outcurve, pre-
serve, reserve, unnerve.

-es. See **-ess.**

-esce. See **-ess.**

-ese. See **-ease.**

-esh, crêche, flesh, fresh, mesh, thresh;
afresh, enmesh, immesh, refresh; Gilga-
mesh.

-esk. See **-esque.**

-esque, desk; burlesque, grotesque; alham-
bresque, arabesque, humoresque, Kafka-
esque, picaresque, picturesque, Roman-
esque, statuesque.

-ess, Bess, bless, cess, chess, cress, dress,
guess, jess, Jess, less, mess, press, stress,
Tess, tress, yes; abscess, access, actress,
address, aggress, assess, caress, compress,
confess, countess, depress, digress, dis-
tress, duress, egress, empress, excess, express, finesse, impress, ingress, largesse,
Loch Ness, mattress, noblesse, obsess,
oneness, oppress, possess, princess, pro-
fess, progress, recess, redress, repress, suc-
cess, suppress, transgress, undress, unless;
acquiesce, baroness, coalesce, comfortless,
convalesce, decompress, dispossess, effer-
vesce, Inverness, obsolesce, opalesce, over-
dress, PMS, politesse, repossess, retrogress,
sorceress, SOS, wilderness; nevertheless.
     Also: many words with the suffix **-ness**
     (as in *smallness,* etc.) and **-less** (as in
     homeless, etc.)

-esse. See **-ess.**

-essed. See **-est.**

-est, best, blest, breast, Brest, chest, crest,

geste, guest, jest, lest, nest, pest, quest,
rest, test, vest, west, wrest, zest; abreast,
arrest, attest, behest, bequest, Celeste, con-
gest, contest, detest, digest, divest, incest,
infest, inquest, invest, Key West, molest,
protest, request, suggest, unblest, unrest;
acid test, alkahest, Almagest, anapest, Bu-
dapest, Everest, manifest, reinvest, second-
best, self-addressed; disinterest.
  Also: **-ess** + **-ed** (as in *pressed*, etc.)
  Also: many superlative forms ending in
  -est (as in *happiest*, etc.)
-et, bet, debt, fret, get, jet, let, Lett, met, net,
pet, Rhett, set, stet, sweat, threat, tret, vet,
wet, whet, yet; abet, aigrette, Annette, ap-
plet, barrette, beget, beset, brochette, bru-
nette, cadet, cassette, Claudette, Colette,
coquette, corvette, curvet, duet, egret, for-
get, gazette, grisette, Hamlet, Jeannette,
octet, offset, omelet, quartet, quintet, re-
gret, rosette, roulette, septet, sestet, sextet,
soubrette, Tibet, upset, vignette; alphabet,
amulet, anisette, banneret, baronet, bassi-
net, bayonet, cabinet, calumet, castanet,
cigarette, clarinet, coronet, epaulet, epithet,
etiquette, Internet, Juliet, marmoset, marti-
net, mignonette, minaret, minuet, neti-
quette, parapet, pirouette, quadruplet,
quintuplet, rivulet, serviette, silhouette,
space cadet, suffragette, tourniquet, vinai-
grette, violet, winterset; marionette, photo-
offset, audiocassette, videocassette.
-etch, etch, fetch, ketch, retch, sketch,
stretch, vetch, wretch; outstretch.
-ete. See **-eat.**
-eth. See **-eath.**

-ette. See **-et.**
-eu. See **-ew.**
-euce. See **-use.**
-eud. See **-ude.**
-eur. See **-er.**
-euth. See **-ooth.**
-eve. See **-eave.**
-ew, blew, blue, boo, brew, chew, clue, coo, coup, crew, cue, dew, do, drew, due, ewe, few, flew, flu, flue, glue, gnu, goo, grew, hew, hue, Hugh, Jew, knew, Lew, lieu, loo, Lou, mew, moo, mu, new, nu, pew, phew, queue, rue, screw, shoe, shrew, skew, slew, slough, sou, spew, stew, strew, sue, Sue, threw, through, to, too, true, two, view, who, woo, yew, you, zoo; accrue, adieu, ado, ague, Ainu, Andrew, Anjou, anew, askew, bamboo, bedew, bijou, cachou, canoe, cashew, cuckoo, curfew, curlew, debut, drive-through, emu, endue, ensue, eschew, Hindu, imbue, issue, juju, Kung fu, menu, mildew, milieu, Peru, pooh-pooh, pursue, purview, ragout, renew, review, shampoo, subdue, taboo, tattoo, tissue, too-too, undo, venue, voodoo, withdrew, wu shu, yahoo, Zulu; avenue, barbecue, billet-doux, catechu, cockatoo, curlicue, déjà vu, gardy loo, interview, kangaroo, misconstrue, parvenu, pas de deux, PDQ, rendezvous, residue, retinue, revenue, toodle-oo, Timbuktu; Kalamazoo, merci beaucoup.
-ewd. See **-ude.**
-ews. See **-ooze** and **-use.**
-ewt. See **-ute.**

-ex, ex, flex, hex, lex, rex, Rex, sex, specs, vex; annex, apex, codex, complex, convex, index, perplex, reflex, Rx, safe sex, spandex, Tex-Mex; circumflex, googolplex, multiplex, unisex.

Also: **-eck** + **-s** (as in *pecks*, etc.)

-exed. See **-ext.**

-ext, next, text; pretext.

Also: **-ex** + **-ed** (as in *vexed*, etc.)

-ey (-ā). See **-ay.**

-ey (-ē). See **-ee.**

-eyed. See **-ade.**

-eys. See **-aze.**

-ez, fez, says; Juarez, malaise, Suez; Marseillaise.

-i (-ē). See **-ee.**

-i (-ī). See **-y.**

-ib, bib, crib, dib, drib, fib, glib, jib, nib, rib, sib, squib; ad-lib, Carib.

-ibe, bribe, gibe, jibe, scribe, tribe; ascribe, describe, imbibe, inscribe, prescribe, proscribe, subscribe, transcribe; circumscribe, diatribe, superscribe.

-ic. See **-ick.**

-ice, bice, Brice, dice, ice, gneiss, lice, mice, nice, price, rice, slice, spice, splice, thrice, trice, twice, vice, vise; advice, allspice, concise, device, entice, precise, suffice; edelweiss, overnice, paradise, sacrifice.

-iced. See **-ist.**

-ich. See **-itch.**

-ick, brick, chic, chick, click, crick, dick, Dick, flick, hick, kick, lick, mick, nick, Nick, pick, prick, quick, rick, sic, sick, slick, snick, stick, thick, tick, trick, Vic,

wick; broomstick, carsick, caustic, gold-
brick, heartsick, lovesick, rubric, seasick,
sputnik, toothpick, triptych, yardstick;
acoustic, arsenic, artistic, bailiwick, Bene-
dick, bishopric, Bolshevik, candlestick,
candlewick, catholic, chivalric, choleric,
double-quick, fiddlestick, heretic, limerick,
lunatic, maverick, Menshevik, pogostick,
politic, Reykjavik, rhetoric, turmeric; arch-
bishopric, arithmetic, cataleptic, impolitic.

-icked. See **-ict.**

-icks. See **-ix.**

-ict, Pict, strict; addict, afflict, conflict, con-
strict, convict, depict, edict, evict, inflict,
predict, restrict; benedict, Benedict, contra-
dict, derelict, interdict.

　　Also: **-ick** + **-ed** (as in *picked,* etc.)

-id, id, bid, chid, Cid, did, grid, hid, kid, lid,
mid, quid, rid, skid, slid, squid; amid, Da-
vid, druid, El Cid, Enid, eyelid, forbid,
gravid, Madrid, nonskid, outbid, outdid,
Ovid, rabid, undid; arachnid, Captain Kidd,
insipid, invalid, katydid, overbid, pyramid,
underbid; caryatid.

-ide, bide, bride, chide, Clyde, glide, guide,
hide, pied, pride, ride, side, slide, snide,
stride, tide, wide; abide, aside, astride,
backside, backslide, beside, bedside, be-
stride, betide, broadside, bromide, carbide,
cockeyed, collide, confide, cowhide, cross-
eyed, decide, deride, divide, elide, green-
eyed, hillside, horsehide, inside, misguide,
noontide, one-eyed, outside, oxide, pop-
eyed, preside, provide, reside, seaside,
subside, sulfide, sun-dried, wall-eyed, way-

side, Yuletide, worldwide; almond-eyed, alongside, bonafide, Christmastide, coincide, dioxide, Eastertide, eventide, fratricide, genocide, homicide, iodide, matricide, monoxide, mountainside, open-eyed, override, parricide, peroxide, regicide, subdivide, suicide, supply-side, underside, waterside, Whitsuntide; formaldehyde, infanticide, insecticide, nucleotide, tyrannicide.

Also: **-ie** + **-d** (as in *lied*, etc.)
Also: **-igh** + **-ed** (as in *sighed*, etc.)
Also: **-y** + **-ed** (as in *cried*, etc.)

-ides, ides; besides.
Also: **-ide** + **-s** (as in *tides, hides,* etc.)

-idge. See **-age** (-ĭj).

-idst, bidst, chidst, didst, hidst, midst, ridst; amidst, forbidst.

-ie (-ē). See **-ee.**

-ie (-ī). See **-y.**

-iece. See **-ease.**

-ied. See **-ide.**

-ief, beef, brief, chief, fief, feoff, grief, leaf, lief, reef, sheaf, thief; belief, fig leaf, relief; bas relief, cloverleaf, disbelief, handkerchief, interleaf, leitmotif, Tenerife, unbelief; apéritif.

-iege, liege, siege; besiege, prestige.

-ield, field, shield, weald, wield, yield; afield, infield, minefield, outfield, Springfield, well-heeled; battlefield, Chesterfield.
Also: **-eal** + **-ed** (as in *healed*, etc.)
Also: **-eel** + **-ed** (as in *peeled*, etc.)

-ien. See **-ean.**

-iend (-ēnd), fiend; archfiend.

Also: **-ean** + **-ed** (as in *cleaned*, etc.)

Also: **-een** + **-ed** (as in *careened*, etc.)

-iend (-end). See **-end.**

-ier (-ēr). See **-eer.**

-ier (-ī^ər). See **-ire.**

-ierce, Bierce, fierce, pierce, tierce; transpierce.

-iest. See **-east.**

-ieu. See **-ew.**

-ieve. See **-eave.**

-iew. See **-ew.**

-ieze. See **-ease.**

-if, biff, cliff, glyph, griff, if, jiff, miff, riff, Riff, skiff, sniff, stiff, tiff, whiff; Cardiff, Heathcliffe, Joseph, mastiff, midriff, plaintiff, pontiff, Radcliffe, serif, sheriff; bindle stiff, handkerchief, hieroglyph, hippogriff, petroglyph, sans serif.

-ife, fife, knife, life, rife, strife, wife; alewife, half-life, housewife, jackknife, loosestrife, lowlife, midlife, midwife; afterlife, Duncan Phyfe, trophy wife.

-iff. See **-if.**

-iffed. See **-ift.**

-ift, drift, gift, grift, lift, rift, shift, shrift, sift, swift, thrift; adrift, airlift, face-lift, festschrift, snowdrift, spendthrift, spindrift, uplift.

Also: **-iff** + **-ed** (as in *whiffed*, etc.)

-ig, big, brig, dig, fig, gig, grig, jig, pig, prig, rig, sprig, swig, trig, twig, Whig, wig; brillig, renege, shindig; infra dig, jury-rig, periwig, thimblerig, whirligig; thingamajig.

-igh. See **-y.**

-ighed. See **-ide.**

-ighs. See **-ize.**

-ight. See **-ite.**

-ign. See **-ine.**

-igned. See **-ind.**

-igue. See **-eague.**

-ike, bike, dike, hike, like, Mike, pike, psych, shrike, spike, tyke; alike, dislike, Klondike, turnpike, unlike, Vandyke; marlinspike.

-il. See **-ill.**

-ilch, filch, milch, pilch, zilch.

-ild (-ĭld), build, gild, guild; rebuild, regild, unchilled, untilled; unfulfilled.
> Also: **-ill** + **-ed** (as in *killed, skilled,* etc.)

-ild (-īld), aisled, child, mild, wild, Wilde.
> Also: **-ile** + **-ed** (as in *filed,* etc.)
> Also: **-yle** + **-ed** (as in *styled,* etc.)

-ile (-īl), aisle, bile, chyle, faille, file, guile, heil, I'll, isle, lisle, mile, Nile, pile, rile, smile, stile, style, tile, vile, Weill, while, wile; anile, Argyle, awhile, beguile, compile, defile, edile, erewhile, exile, gentile, meanwhile, revile, senile, servile; Anglophile, crocodile, domicile, Francophile, infantile, juvenile, mercantile, oenophile, puerile, reconcile, Slavophile; aileurophile, bibliophile, Germanophile.

-ile (-ēl). See **-eal.**

-ile (-ĭl). See **-ill.**

-iled. See **-ild.**

-ilk, bilk, ilk, milk, silk.

-ill, bill, Bill, brill, chill, dill, drill, fill, frill, gill, grill, hill, ill, Jill, kill, mill, nil, Phil, pill, quill, rill, shill, shrill, sill, skill, spill, squill, still, swill, thill, thrill, 'til, till, trill,

twill, 'twill, will, Will; Brazil, distil, down-
hill, fulfill, instill, quadrille, Seville, tread-
mill, uphill; chlorophyll, codicil, daffodil,
domicile, espadrille, imbecile, Louisville,
versatile, volatile, whippoorwill, Yggdrasil.

-ille (-ēl). See **-eal**.

-ille (-il). See **-ill**.

-illed. See **-ild**.

-ilt, built, gilt, guilt, hilt, jilt, kilt, lilt, milt,
quilt, silt, spilt, stilt, tilt, wilt; atilt, rebuilt;
Vanderbilt.

-ilth, filth, spilth, tilth.

-im, brim, dim, glim, grim, Grimm, gym,
him, hymn, Jim, Kim, limb, limn, prim,
rim, shim, skim, slim, swim, Tim, trim,
vim, whim; bedim, paynim, prelim, Purim;
acronym, antonym, cherubim, eponym,
homonym, interim, paradigm, pseudonym,
seraphim, synonym.

-imb (-im). See **-im**.

-imb (-īm). See **-ime**.

-ime, chime, chyme, climb, clime, crime,
cyme, dime, grime, I'm, lime, mime,
prime, rhyme, rime, slime, thyme, time;
begrime, bedtime, daytime, lifetime, mean-
time, sometime, springtime, sublime; Gug-
genheim, maritime, overtime, pantomime,
paradigm, summertime, wintertime.

-imes, betimes, ofttimes, sometimes; often-
times.
    Also: **-ime** + **-s** (as in *crimes*, etc.)
    Also: **-yme** + **-s** (as in *rhymes*, etc.)

-imp, blimp, chimp, crimp, gimp, guimpe,
imp, limp, pimp, primp, scrimp, shrimp,
simp, skimp, wimp.

-impse, glimpse.

Also: **-imp** + **-s** (as in *skimps*, etc.)

-in, been, bin, chin, din, djinn, fin, Finn, gin, grin, in, inn, jinn, kin, pin, shin, sin, skin, spin, thin, tin, twin, whin, win; akin, bearskin, begin, Berlin, bowfin, Brooklyn, buckskin, carbine, chagrin, Corinne, herein, sidespin, tailspin, therein; alkaline, aniline, aquiline, aspirin, crinoline, crystalline, discipline, endorphin, feminine, gelatin, genuine, glycerine, harlequin, heroine, Jacobin, javelin, jessamine, Lohengrin, mandarin, mandolin, mannequin, masculine, Mickey Finn, moccasin, paladin, peregrine, saccharin, sibylline, violin, Zeppelin; adrenalin, Alexandrine, elephantine.

-inc. See **-ink.**

-ince, blintz, chintz, mince, prince, quince, rinse, since, wince; convince, evince.

Also: **-int** + **-s** (as in *prints*, etc.)

-inch, chinch, cinch, clinch, finch, flinch, inch, lynch, pinch, winch; chaffinch, goldfinch.

-inct, tinct; distinct, extinct, instinct, precinct, succinct; indistinct.

Also: **-ink** + **-ed** (as in *winked*, etc.)

-ind (-īnd), bind, blind, find, grind, hind, kind, mind, rind, wind; behind, mankind, purblind, remind, unkind, unwind; colorblind, humankind, mastermind, undersigned, womankind.

Also: **-ign** + **-ed** (as in *signed*, etc.)

Also: **-ine** + **-ed** (as in *dined*, etc.)

-ind (-ind), Ind, wind; rescind, whirlwind,

woodwind; Amerind, tamarind.

Also: **-in** + **-ed** (as in *grinned*, etc.)

-ine (-īn), brine, chine, dine, fine, kine, line, mine, nine, pine, Rhine, shine, shrine, sign, sine, spine, spline, stein, swine, syne, thine, tine, trine, twine, vine, whine, wine; airline, align, assign, benign, bovine, canine, carbine, carmine, combine, condign, confine, consign, decline, define, design, divine, enshrine, entwine, feline, grapevine, hircine, Holstein, incline, lifeline, lupine, mainline, malign, moonshine, opine, outshine, ovine, railline, recline, refine, repine, resign, saline, sunshine, supine, vulpine, woodbine; Adeline, alkaline, androgyne, anodyne, Apennine, aquiline, Argentine, asinine, bottom line, Byzantine, calcimine, calomine, Caroline, Clementine, columbine, concubine, disincline, eglantine, etamine, Florentine, interline, intertwine, iodine, leonine, Liechtenstein, palatine, porcupine, saturnine, serpentine, superfine, timberline, Turnverein, turpentine, underline, undermine, valentine, waterline; elephantine.

-ine (-ēn). See **-ean.**

-ine (-in). See **-in.**

-ined. See **-ind.**

-ing, bing, bring, cling, ding, fling, king, Ming, ping, ring, sing, sling, spring, sting, string, swing, Synge, thing, wing, wring, ying; evening, hireling, mainspring, O-ring, plaything, something, unsling, unstring; anything, atheling, everything, opening, underling.

Also: participles in **-ing** and gerunds (as *clamoring*, etc.)

-inge, binge, cringe, fringe, hinge, Inge, singe, springe, swinge, tinge, twinge; challenge, impinge, infringe, orange, scavenge, syringe, unhinge.

-ingue. See **-ang.**

-ink, blink, brink, chink, clink, drink, fink, ink, kink, link, mink, pink, rink, shrink, sink, skink, slink, stink, think, wink, zinc; doublethink, hoodwink, lip-sync; bobolink Humperdinck, interlink, Maeterlinck, tiddlywink.

-inked. See **-inct.**

-inks. See **-inx.**

-inned. See **-ind.**

-inse. See **-ince.**

-int, dint, flint, glint, Gynt, hint, lint, mint, print, quint, splint, sprint, squint, stint, tint; asquint, footprint, imprint, misprint, reprint, spearmint; aquatint, peppermint; septuagint.

-inth, plinth; absinthe, Corinth; hyacinth, labyrinth, terebinth.

-ints. See **-ince.**

-inx, jinx, lynx, minx, sphinx; larynx, methinks, salpinx; tiddlywinks.

Also: **-ink** + **-s** (as in *thinks*, etc.)

-ip, blip, chip, clip, dip, drip, flip, grip, grippe, gyp, hip, kip, lip, nip, pip, quip, rip, scrip, ship, sip, skip, slip, snip, strip, tip, trip, whip, yip, zip; airstrip, catnip, cowslip, equip, flagship, horsewhip, lightship, outstrip, transship, unzip, V-chip; battleship, ego trip, microchip, underlip, weatherstrip.

Also: words with **-ship** as suffix (as *fellowship, scholarship*, etc.)

-ipe, gripe, pipe, ripe, snipe, stipe, stripe, swipe, tripe, type, wipe; bagpipe, blowpipe, hornpipe, pitchpipe, sideswipe, tintype, unripe, windpipe; archetype, collotype, guttersnipe, Linotype, Monotype, overripe, prototype; Daguerrotype, electrotype, stereotype.

-ipse, eclipse, ellipse; apocalypse.

Also: **-ip** + **-s** (as in *chips*, etc.)

-ipt, crypt, script, conscript, encrypt, postscript, transcript.

Also: **-ip** + **-ped** (as in *tipped*, etc.)

-ique. See **-eak.**

-ir. See **-er.**

-irch. See **-urch.**

-ird. See **-urd.**

-ire (-ī^ər). briar, brier, buyer, choir, dire, fire, flyer, friar, gyre, hire, ire, liar, lyre, mire, plier, prior, pyre, quire, shire, sire, spire, squire, tire, Tyre, wire; acquire, admire, afire, aspire, attire, bemire, bonfire, conspire, desire, empire, enquire, entire, esquire, expire, grandsire, hot-wire, inquire, inspire, perspire, quagmire, require, respire, retire, sapphire, satire, spitfire, transpire, vampire, wildfire.

Also: **-y** + **-er** (as in *crier, modifier*, etc.) See also: **-ier.**

-irge. See **-erge.**

-irk. See **-urk.**

-irl. See **-url.**

-irm, berm, firm, germ, sperm, squirm, term,

worm; affirm, bookworm, confirm, glow-
worm, grubworm, infirm; isotherm, pachy-
derm, reaffirm.

-irp. See **-urp.**

-irr. See **-er.**

-irred. See **-urd.**

-irst. See **-urst.**

-irt. See **-ert.**

-irth, berth, birth, dearth, earth, firth, girth,
mirth, Perth, worth; stillbirth, unearth.

-is (-iz), biz, fizz, friz, his, is, Liz, Ms., quiz,
'tis, viz, whiz, wiz; Cadiz, show biz.

-is (-is). See **-iss.**

-ise (-īs). See **-ice.**

-ise (-īz). See **-ize.**

-ish, dish, fish, Gish, knish, pish, squish,
swish, wish; anguish, bluefish, flatfish,
goldfish, whitefish, whitish; angelfish, ba-
byish, devilfish, devilish, feverish, flying
fish, gibberish, kittenish, microfiche; im-
poverish.
   Also: words with **-ish** as suffix (as *childish, sluggish,* etc.)

-isk, bisque, brisk, disc, disk, frisk, risk,
whisk; asterisk, basilisk, obelisk, oda-
lisque, tamarisk; videodisk.

-ism, chrism, prism, schism; abysm, Babism,
baptism, Buddhism, Chartism, deism, fad-
dism, Fascism, Grecism, Jainism, Mah-
dism, monism, mutism, psellism, purism,
sadism, snobbism, sophism, Sufism, tech-
nism, theism, truism, Whiggism, Yogism;
absinthism, actinism, acrotism, albinism,
algorism, altruism, amorphism, anarchism,
aneurysm, Anglicism, animism, aphorism,

archaism, asterism, atavism, atheism, atomism, Atticism, barbarism, Biblicism, Bolshevism, botulism, Brahminism, Briticism, Britishism, brutalism, Byronism, cabalism, Caesarism, Calvinism, carnalism, cataclysm, catechism, Celticism, centralism, chauvinism, classicism, cocainism, Cockneyism, Communism, cretinism, criticism, cynicism, daltonism, dandyism, Darwinism, demonism, despotism, dimorphism, ditheism, dogmatism, dowdyism, Druidism, dualism, dynamism, egoism, egotism, embolism, erethism, ergotism, euphemism, euphonism, euphuism, exorcism, extremism, fatalism, feminism, fetishism, feudalism, fogyism, foreignism, formalism, formulism, Gallicism, galvanism, gentilism, Germanism, giantism, gigantism, gnosticism, Gothicism, grundyism, heathenism, Hebraism, hedonism, Hellenism, helotism, heroism, Hinduism, humanism, humorism, hypnotism, Jansenism, jingoism, journalism, Judaism, laconism, Lamaism, lambdacism, Latinism, legalism, Leninism, localism, Lollardism, loyalism, magnetism, mannerism, martialism, masochism, mechanism, Menshevism, mephitism, mesmerism, Methodism, microcosm, Mithraism, modernism, monadism, moralism, Mormonism, morphinism, Moslemism, mysticism, narcotism, nepotism, nihilism, occultism, onanism, organism, optimism, ostracism, pacifism, paganism, pantheism, paroxysm, Parseeism, pauperism, pessimism, pietism, Platonism, pluralism, pragmatism, prognathism, prosaism, pyrrhonism, Quakerism, quietism, quixotism, Rabbinism, racialism, realism, regalism, rheumatism, Romanism, rowdyism, royalism, ruralism, satanism, Saxonism, schematism, scientism, Semitism, Shakerism, shamanism, Shintoism, sigmatism, Sinicism, skepticism, Socialism, solecism, solipsism, specialism, spiritism, spoonerism, Stalinism, stoicism, suffragism, syllogism, symbolism, synchronism, syncretism, synergism, tantalism, Taoism, terrorism, toadyism, Toryism, totemism, traumatism, tribalism, tritheism, ultraism, unionism, vandalism, verbalism, vocalism, volcanism, voodooism, vulgarism, vulpinism, witticism, Yankeeism, Zionism; absenteeism, absolutism, achromatism, aestheticism, agnosticism, alcoholism, alienism, allotropism, amateurism, anabolism, anachronism, Anglicanism, antagonism, Arianism, asceticism, astigmatism, autochthonism, automatism, bimetallism, Byzantinism, cannibalism, capitalism, catabolism, Catholicism, charlatanism, clericalism, collectivism, commercialism, communalism, Confucianism, conservatism, democratism, determinism, diabolism, dilletantism, eclecticism, empiricism, eroticism, evangelism, expressionism, externalism, fanaticism, favoritism, federalism, generalism, Hibernicism, Hispanicism, hooliganism, hyperbolism, idealism, idiotism, impressionism, invalidism, isochronism, isomerism, isomorphism, isotropism, Jacobinism, Jacobitism, Jesuitism, katabolism, laconicism, legitimism, liberalism, libertinism, literalism,

Lutheranism, malapropism, mercantilism, metabolism, metachronism, militarism, moderatism, monasticism, monotheism, mutualism, narcoticism, nationalism, naturalism, negativism, neologism, nicotinism, noctambulism, nominalism, objectivism, obscurantism, obstructionism, officialism, opportunism, parallelism, parasitism, paternalism, patriotism, pedagogism, Pharisaism, Philistinism, philosophism, plagiarism, plebianism, polymerism, polymorphism, polyphonism, polytheism, positivism, probabilism, progressivism, Protestantism, provincialism, Puritanism, radicalism, rationalism, recidivism, regionalism, ritualism, romanticism, ruffianism, Sadduceeism, scholasticism, secessionism, sectionalism, secularism, sensualism, separatism, Shavianism, somnambulism, somniloquism, subjectivism, sycophantism, syndicalism, theosophism, universalism, ventriloquism, Wesleyanism; abolitionism, agrarianism, Americanism, anthropomorphism, Bohemianism, Cartesianism, colloquialism, colonialism, conceptualism, conventionalism, cosmopolitism, equestrianism, evolutionism, existentialism, heliotropism, hermaphroditism, heteromorphism, Hibernianism, histrionicism, imperialism, incendiarism, indeterminism, indifferentism, industrialism, Manicheanism, materialism, medievalism, Mohammedanism, Occidentalism, Orientalism, parochialism, phenomenalism, postimpressionism, professionalism, proverbialism, Republicanism, Rosicrucianism, sacerdotalism, sectarianism, sensa-

tionalism, sentimentalism, Spencerianism,
spiritualism, theatricalism, Tractarianism,
traditionalism, transmigrationism, Utopian-
ism, vernacularism; antinomianism, anti-
quarianism, ceremonialism, Congregation-
alism, constitutionalism, cosmospolitanism,
experimentalism, individualism, intellectu-
alism, internationalism, presbyterianism,
preternaturalism, proletarianism, supernat-
uralism, Unitarianism, vegetarianism; Aris-
totelianism, humanitarianism, utilitarian-
ism; antidisestablishmentarianism.

-isp, crisp, lisp, wisp; will o' the wisp.

-iss, bliss, Chris, dis, hiss, kiss, miss, Swiss,
this; abyss, amiss, crevice, dismiss, jaun-
dice, remiss; ambergris, armistice, artifice,
avarice, Beatrice, benefice, chrysalis, cow-
ardice, dentrifice, edifice, emphasis, gene-
sis, nemesis, orifice, precipice, prejudice,
synthesis, verdigris; acropolis, anabasis,
analysis, antithesis, dieresis, hypothesis,
metropolis, necropolis, paralysis, parenthe-
sis, rigor mortis; metamorphosis; abiogene-
sis.

-ist (-ist), cist, cyst, fist, gist, grist, hist!, list,
mist, schist, tryst, twist, whist, wist, wrist;
artist, assist, Baptist, blacklist, Buddhist,
chartist, chemist, consist, Cubist, cueist,
cyclist, deist, dentist, desist, druggist, duel-
ist, enlist, entwist, exist, faddist, Fascist,
flautist, florist, flutist, harpist, hymnist, in-
sist, jurist, linguist, lutist, lyrist, metrist,
monist, palmist, persist, psalmist, purist,
resist, sacrist, simplist, sophist, statist, styl-
ist, subsist, theist, Thomist, tourist, Trap-
pist, tropist, typist; alarmist, alchemist, al-

gebrist, Alpinist, altruist, amethyst, amorist, analyst, anarchist, animist, annalist, aorist, aphorist, Arabist, archivist, armorist, atheist, atomist, balloonist, banjoist, biblicist, bicyclist, bigamist, Bolshevist, botanist, canoeist, cartoonist, casuist, catalyst, catechist, centralist, chauvinist, choralist, citharist, classicist, coexist, colloquist, colonist, colorist, Communist, conformist, copyist, Calvinist, cymbalist, Darwinist, diarist, dogmatist, Donatist, dramatist, dualist, egoist, egotist, elegist, essayist, Eucharist, eulogist, euphuist, extremist, fabulist, factionist, fatalist, feminist, fetishist, feudalist, fictionist, folklorist, formalist, futurist, guitarist, Hebraist, hedonist, Hellenist, herbalist, hobbyist, homilist, humanist, humorist, hypnotist, intertwist, Jansenist, journalist, Judaist, lampoonist, Latinist, legalist, librettist, liturgist, lobbyist, loyalist, machinist, martialist, mechanist, medallist, mesmerist, Methodist, Mithraist, modernist, monarchist, moralist, motorist, nepotist, Nihilist, novelist, occultist, oculist, ophthalmist, optimist, organist, pacifist, pantheist, papalist, pessimist, pharmacist, physicist, pianist, pietist, Platonist, pluralist, portraitist, pragmatist, pre-exist, publicist, pugilist, pyrrhonist, realist, re-enlist, reformist, repealist, reservist, rhapsodist, Romanist, ruralist, satirist, scientist, sciolist, Shamanist, Shintoist, Socialist, solecist, soloist, specialist, Stalinist, strategist, suffragist, symbolist, Talmudist, Taoist, terrorist, theorist, trombonist, Trotskyist, unionist, Vedantist, violist, vocalist, Zionist, zitherist; absolutist, accompanist, agronomist, algebraist, alienist, Anabaptist, anatomist, antagonist, anthologist, apiarist, apologist, automatist, autonomist, aviarist, bimetallist, biologist, capitalist, chiropodist, clarinetist, clericalist, collectivist, commercialist, communalist, concessionist, contortionist, determinist, diplomatist, dramaturgist, economist, empiricist, enamelist, equilibrist, ethnologist, Evangelist, exclusionist, expressionist, extortionist, Federalist, geologist, geometrist, horologist, hygienist, hyperbolist, idealist, illusionist, impressionist, legitimist, liberalist, literalist, lycanthropist, manicurist, meliorist, metallurgist, militarist, misanthropist, misogamist, misogynist, monogamist, monologist, monopolist, monotheist, necrologist, negationist, negativist, neologist, neuropathist, noctambulist, Nominalist, nonconformist, objectivist, obscurantist, obstructionist, ocularist, opportunist, optometrist, parachutist, pathologist, perfectionist, philanthropist, philatelist, philogynist, phrenologist, plagiarist, polemicist, polygamist, pomologist, positivist, propagandist, protagonist, protectionist, psychiatrist, psychologist, psychopathist, rationalist, recidivist, religionist, revisionist, revivalist, ritualist, salvationist, secessionist, secularist, sensualist, separatist, soliloquist, somnambulist, somniloquist, spectroscopist, symbologist, syndicalist, synonymist, taxidermist, taxonomist, telepathist, telephonist, thaumaturgist, theologist, theosophist, therapeutist, tobacconist, traditionist, ventriloquist, violinist; abolitionist, agriculturist, anthropologist, anthropomorphist, archæologist, automobilist, caricaturist, coalitionist, conceptionalist, conceptualist, constitutionist, dermatologist, Egyptologist, elocutionist, emigrationist, encyclopedist, entomologist, etymologist, evolutionist, federationist, floriculturist, genealogist, gynecologist, horticulturist, imperialist, insurrectionist, medievalist, melodramatist, mineralogist, miniaturist, monometallist, Occidentalist, ophthalmologist, oppositionist, Orientalist, osteopathist, pharmacologist, phenomenalist, physiologist, postimpressionist, preferentialist, prohibitionist, revolutionist, sacerdotalist, spiritualist, traditionalist, transcendentalist, universalist, violoncellist, vivisectionist; arboriculturist, bacteriologist, ceremonialist, Congregationalist, constitutionalist, controversialist, conversationalist, educationalist, experimentalist, individualist, institutionalist, internationalist, supernaturalist.

    Also: **-iss** + **-ed** (as in *missed*, etc.)

-ist (-īst), Christ, feist; Zeitgeist; poltergeist.

    Also: **-ice** + **-ed** (as in *sliced*, etc.)

-it, bit, bitt, chit, fit, flit, grit, hit, it, kit, knit, lit, mitt, nit, pit, Pitt, quit, sit, skit, slit, smit, spit, split, sprit, tit, twit, whit, wit, writ, zit; acquit, admit, armpit, befit, bowsprit, commit, emit, hobbit, misfit, moonlit, omit, outwit, permit, refit, remit, respite, starlit, submit, sunlit, tidbit, tomtit, transmit, unfit; apposite, benefit, counterfeit, definite, exquisite, favorite, hypocrite,

infinite, Jesuit, opposite, perquisite, preter-
ite, requisite; indefinite.

-itch, bitch, ditch, fitch, flitch, hitch, itch,
niche, pitch, rich, snitch, stitch, switch,
twitch, which, witch; bewitch, enrich,
hemstitch, unhitch; czarevitch.

-ite (-īt), bight, bite, blight, bright, byte, cite,
dight, Dwight, fight, flight, fright, height,
hight, kite, knight, light, might, mite,
night, plight, quite, right, rite, sight, site,
sleight, slight, smite, spite, sprite, tight,
trite, white, wight, wright, write; affright,
alight, aright, bedight, benight, bobwhite,
contrite, daylight, delight, despite, down-
right, dunnite, excite, foresight, forthright,
goodnight, headlight, Hittite, hoplite, ig-
nite, incite, indict, indite, invite, midnight,
moonlight, outright, polite, recite, requite,
samite, Shiite, starlight, sunlight, tonight,
twilight, unite, upright, wainwright, wheel-
wright; acolyte, aconite, anchorite, anthra-
cite, appetite, blatherskite, Canaanite, can-
dlelight, copyright, disunite, dynamite,
erudite, eremite, expedite, fahrenheit, Ge-
sundheit, Hepplewhite, impolite, kilobyte,
Moabite, Muscovite, neophyte, overnight,
oversight, parasite, plebiscite, proselyte,
recondite, satellite, stalactite, stalagmite,
troglodyte, underwrite, vulcanite, water-
sprite, watertight, weathertight, Yemenite;
electrolyte, gemütlichkeit, hermaphrodite,
Israelite, meteorite, suburbanite; Pre-
Raphaelite.

-ite (-it). See **-it.**
-ites (-its). See **-itz.**

-ith, frith, kith, myth, pith, smith, with; Edith, forthwith, herewith, therewith, wherewith, zenith; acrolith, Arrowsmith, Granny Smith, monolith, otolith, silver-smith.

-ithe, blithe, lithe, scythe, tithe, withe, writhe.

-itz, blitz, ditz, Fritz, grits, Ritz, spitz.
     Also: **-it** + **-s** (as in *bits,* etc.)
     Also: **-ite** + **-s** (as in *favorites,* etc.)

-ive (-īv), chive, Clive, dive, drive, five, gyve, hive, I've, live, rive, shive, shrive, strive, thrive, wive; alive, archive, arrive, beehive, connive, contrive, deprive, derive, nosedive, ogive, revive, survive, test-drive; overdrive.

-ive (-iv), give, live, sieve, spiv; active, captive, costive, cursive, dative, fictive, forgive, furtive, massive, missive, motive, native, outlive, passive, pensive, plaintive, relive, restive, sportive, suasive, votive; ablative, abortive, abrasive, absorptive, abstersive, abstractive, abusive, adaptive, additive, adductive, adhesive, adjective, adjunctive, adoptive, affective, afflictive, aggressive, allusive, amative, arrestive, aspersive, assertive, assuasive, assumptive, attentive, attractive, causative, coercive, cognitive, cohesive, collective, collusive, combative, combustive, compulsive, conative, conceptive, concessive, concussive, conclusive, concoctive, conducive, conductive, conflictive, congestive, conjunctive, connective, constrictive, constructive, consultive, consumptive, contractive, convulsive, corrective, corrosive, corruptive, creative, curative, deceptive, decisive, deductive, defective, defensive, delusive, depictive, depressive, derisive, descriptive, destructive, detective, detractive, diffusive, digestive, digressive, directive, discursive, disjunctive, disruptive, dissuasive, distinctive, distractive, divertive, divisive, divulsive, effective, effusive, elective, elusive, emissive, emotive, emulsive, evasive, excessive, exclusive, excursive, exhaustive, expansive, expensive, expletive, explosive, expressive, expulsive, extensive, extortive, extractive, extrusive, fixative, formative, fugitive, genitive, gerundive, hortative, illusive, impassive, impressive, impulsive, inactive, incentive, incisive, inclusive, incursive, inductive, infective, inflective, infusive, ingestive, inscriptive, instinctive, instructive, intensive, intrusive, invective, inventive, laudative, laxative, lenitive, locative, lucrative, narrative, negative, nutritive, objective, obstructive, obtrusive, offensive, olfactive, oppressive, optative, partitive, perceptive, percussive, perfective, permissive, perspective, persuasive, pervasive, positive, possessive, preclusive, precursive, predictive, pre-emptive, prescriptive, presumptive, preventive, primitive, privative, productive, progressive, projective, propulsive, proscriptive, prospective, protective, protractive, protrusive, punitive, purgative, purposive, reactive, receptive, recessive, redemptive, reductive, reflective, reflexive, regressive, relative, remissive, repressive, repulsive, respective, responsive, restrictive, resumptive, retentive, retractive, revulsive, secretive, sedative, seductive, selective, sensitive, siccative, subjective, subjunctive, submissive, substantive, subtractive, subversive, successive, suggestive, suppressive, talkative, tentative, transgressive, transitive, transmissive, vibrative, vindictive, vocative; abrogative, accusative, acquisitive, admonitive, adumbrative, affirmative, alternative, appellative, attributive, augmentative, calculative, circumscriptive, circumventive, coextensive, combinative, comparative, compensative, competitive, compositive, comprehensive, connotative, consecutive, conservative, contemplative, contributive, conversative, corporative, correlative, counteractive, cumulative, declarative, decorative, dedicative, definitive, demonstrative, denotative, deprecative, derivative, diminutive, disputative, distributive, educative, evocative, excitative, exclamative, execrative, executive, exhibitive, exhortative, expectative, explicative, explorative, expositive, figurative, generative, germinative, hesitative, illustrative, imitative, imperative, imperceptive, inattentive, incohesive, inconclusive, indecisive, indicative, indistinctive, ineffective, inexhaustive, inexpansive, inexpensive, inexpressive, infinitive, informative, innovative, inoffensive, inquisitive, insensitive, integrative, intransitive, introductive, introspective, intuitive, irrespective, irresponsive, irritative, iterative, judicative, legislative, locomotive, mediative medicative, meditative, nominative, operative, palliative, pejorative, preparative, prerogative, preservative, preventative, procreative, prohibitive, provocative, putrefactive, qualitative, quantitative, radiative, rarefactive, reconstructive, recreative, regulative, remonstrative, repetitive, reprehensive, reprobative, reproductive, retroactive, retrogressive, retrospective, ruminative, speculative, stupefactive, superlative, suppurative, vegetative, vindicative; accumulative, administrative, agglutinative, alleviative, alliterative, appreciative, argumentative, assimilative, associative, authoritative, coagulative, commemorative, commiserative, communicative, confederative, cooperative, corroborative, deliberative, depreciative, discriminative, exonerative, expostulative, imaginative, initiative, inoperative, interpretative, interrogative, investigative, irradiative, manipulative, recuperative, reiterative, remunerative, representative, retaliative, significative, subordinative, vituperative; incommunicative, philoprogenitive.

-ix, fix, mix, nix, pyx, six, Styx; admix, affix, commix, helix, infix, matrix, onyx, prefix, prolix, suffix, transfix, unfix; cicatrix, crucifix, fiddlesticks, intermix, politics; double helix, executrix; archaeopteryx.

Also: **-ick** + **-s** (as in *bricks, sticks,* etc.)

-ixed. See **-ixt.**

-ixt, twixt; betwixt.

Also: **-ix** + **-ed** (as in *mixed,* etc.)

-iz. See **-is.**

-ize, guise, prize, rise, size, wise; advise, apprise, arise, assize, baptize, capsize, chastise, comprise, demise, despise, devise, disguise, incise, likewise, misprize, moonrise, revise, sunrise, surmise, surprise, unwise; advertise, aggrandize, agonize, alkalize, amortize, Anglicize, atomize, authorize, barbarize, bastardize, bowdlerize, brutalize, canalize, canonize, carbonize, catechize, cauterize, centralize, circumcise, civilize, classicize, colonize, compromise, criticize, crystallize, deputize, dogmatize, dramatize, emphasize, energize, enterprise, equalize, eulogize, euphemize, exercise, exorcise, feminize, fertilize, feudalize, focalize, formalize, fossilize, fractionize, fraternize, Gallicize, galvanize, Germanize, glutinize, harmonize, Hellenize, humanize, hybridize, hypnotize, idolize, immunize, improvise, ionize, itemize, jazzercize, jeopardize, Judaize, laicize, Latinize, legalize, lionize, liquidize, localize, magnetize, martyrize, maximize, mechanize, memorize, mercerize, mesmerize, metallize, methodize, minimize, mobilize, modernize, monetize, moralize, nasalize, neutralize, normalize, organize, ostracize, otherwise, oxidize, patronize, penalize, pluralize, polarize, polemize, pulverize, realize, recognize, rhapsodize, Romanize, ruralize, satirize, scandalize, schematize, scrutinize, sermonize, signalize, socialize, solemnize, specialize, stabilize, standardize, sterilize, stigmatize, subsidize, summarize, supervise, symbolize, sympathize, symphonize, synchronize, synthesize, systemize, tantalize, televise, temporize, terrorize, theorize, totalize, tranquilize, tyrannize, unionize, utilize, vaporize, verbalize, victimize, vitalize, vocalize, vulcanize, vulgarize, Westernize; acclimatize, actualize, allegorize, alphabetize, anæsthetize, anatomize, antagonize, anthologize, apologize, apostatize, apostrophize, capitalize, catholicize, characterize, Christianize, commercialize, decentralize, dehumanize, demobilize, democratize, demoralize, deodorize, disorganize, economize, epitomize, extemporize, federalize, generalize, hydrogenize, hypothesize, idealize, immobilize, immortalize, italicize, legitimize, liberalize, metabolize, militarize, monopolize, nationalize, naturalize, parenthesize, personalize, philosophize, plagiarize, popularize, prioritize, proselytize, rationalize, regularize, reorganize, ritualize, singularize, soliloquize, systematize, theologize, theosophize, visualize, ventriloquize; Americanize, anathematize, apotheosize, departmentalize, familiarize, legitimatize, materialize, memorialize, particularize, republicanize, revolutionize, secularize, sentimentalize, spiritualize, universalize; constitutionalize, individualize, institutionalize, intellectualize, internationalize.

Also: **-y** + **-s** (as in *testifies*, etc.)
Also: **-eye** + **-s** (as in *eyes*, etc.)
Also: **-igh** + **-s** (as in *sighs*, etc.)

-o (-ō). See **-ow.**

-o (-o͞o). See **-oo.**

-oach, broach, brooch, coach, loach, poach, roach; abroach, approach, cockroach, encroach, reproach.

-oad (-ôd). See **-aud.**

-oad (-ōd). See **-ode.**

-oaf, loaf, oaf; meatloaf; sugarloaf.

-oak. See **-oke.**

-oaks. See **-oax.**

-oal. See **-ole.**

-oaled. See **-old.**

-oam. See **-ome.**

-oan. See **-one.**

-oap. See **-ope.**

-oar. See **-ore.**

-oard. See **-ord.**

-oared. See **-ord.**

-oast. See **-ost.**

-oat. See **-ote.**

-oath. See **-oth.**

-oax, coax, hoax.
    Also: **-oak** + **-s** (as in *cloaks*, etc.)
    Also: **-oke** + **-s** (as in *jokes*, etc.)

-ob, blob, bob, Bob, cob, Cobb, fob, glob, gob, hob, job, knob, lob, mob, nob, rob, slob, snob, sob, squab, swab, throb; corn-cob, heartthrob, hobnob, kabob, macabre, nabob; thingumabob.

-obe, daube, globe, Job, lobe, probe, robe, strobe; conglobe, disrobe, enrobe, microbe, unrobe; Anglophobe, Francophobe, Gallophobe, Russophobe, Slavophobe, xeno-phobe.

-ock, Bach, Bloch, block, bock, chock, clock, cock, crock, doc, dock, flock, frock, hock, jock, Jock, knock, loch, lock, Mach, mock, pock, roc, rock, shock, smock, sock, stock; ad hoc, Balzac, Bangkok, deadlock, Dvo-rak, fetlock, Hancock, hemlock, padlock, peacock, petcock, Rorschach, shamrock, Sherlock, shock jock, Shylock, tick-tock, unfrock, unlock, wedlock, woodcock; alpenstock, antilock, Antioch, hollyhock, Jabberwock, Little Rock, monadnock, Offenbach, poppycock, shuttlecock, weathercock.

-ocked. See **-oct.**

-ocks. See **-ox.**

-oct, concoct, decoct, entr'acte; shellshocked.

Also: **-ock** + **-ed** (as in *flocked,* etc.)

-od, clod, cod, god, hod, nod, odd, plod, pod, prod, quad, quod, rod, scrod, shod, sod, squad, tod, trod, wad; aubade, ballade, Cape Cod, couvade, facade, jihad, Nimrod, roughshod, roulade, slipshod, unshod, untrod; decapod, demigod, goldenrod, lycopod, promenade; Scheherazade.

-ode, bode, code, goad, load, lode, mode, node, ode, road, rode, Spode, strode, toad, woad; abode, anode, cathode, commode, corrode, erode, explode, implode, forebode, geode, implode, payload, railroad, reload, unload, zip code; à la mode, discommode, episode, overload, pigeon-toed.

Also: **-ow** + **-ed** (as in *towed,* etc.)

-odge, dodge, hodge, lodge, podge, stodge; dislodge, hodgepodge.

-oe (-ō). See **-ow.**

-oe (-o͞o). See **-ew.**

-oes (-ōz). See **-ose.**

-oes (-uz). See **-uzz.**

-off, cough, doff, off, scoff, soph, trough; Chekhov, Khrushchev, takeoff; Gorbachev,

Molotov, Nabokov, philosophe. See also
-aff.

-offed. See **-oft.**

-oft, croft, loft, oft, soft; aloft, hayloft; under-
croft.

  Also: **-off** + **-ed** (as in *doffed,* etc.)

  Also: **-ough** + **-ed** (as in *coughed,* etc.)

-og, bog, clog, cog, dog, flog, fog, frog, Gog,
grog, hog, jog, log, nog, Prague, slog;
agog, bulldog, eggnog, incog, Magog, un-
clog, warthog; analogue, catalogue, deca-
logue, demagogue, dialogue, epilogue,
monologue, pedagogue, pettifog, syna-
gogue, travelogue.

-ogue (-ōg), brogue, rogue, vogue; prorogue;
disembogue.

-ogue (-og). See **-og.**

-oice, choice, Joyce, voice; invoice, rejoice,
Rolls Royce.

-oiced. See **-oist.**

-oid, Floyd, Freud, Lloyd, void; avoid, de-
void, ovoid, steroid, tabloid; alkaloid, aner-
oid, anthropoid, asteroid, celluloid, Mon-
goloid, Polaroid, trapezoid; paraboloid.

  Also: **-oy** + **-ed** (as in *enjoyed,* etc.)

-oil, boil, broil, coil, foil, Hoyle, moil, oil,
roil, soil, spoil, toil; despoil, embroil, gum-
boil, parboil, recoil, tinfoil, trefoil, turmoil,
uncoil; hydrofoil, quatrefoil.

-oin, coign, coin, groin, join, loin, quoin; ad-
join, benzoin, Burgoyne, conjoin, Des
Moines, disjoin, enjoin, purloin, rejoin, sirloin, subjoin; tenderloin.

-oint, joint, point; anoint, appoint, aroint,
ballpoint, conjoint, disjoint, dry-point,

West Point; counterpoint, disappoint, nee-
dlepoint, petit point.

-oise, noise, poise; turquoise; counterpoise,
equipoise, Illinois, Iroquois; avoirdupois.
Also: **-oy** + **-s** (as in *toys,* etc.)

-oist, foist, hoist, joist, moist.
Also: **-oice** + **-ed** (as in *voiced,* etc.)

-oit, coit, doit, quoit; adroit, Beloit, dacoit,
Detroit, exploit, introit; maladroit.

-oke, bloke, broke, choke, cloak, coke, Coke,
croak, folk, joke, oak, oke, poke, smoke,
soak, spoke, stroke, toque, woke,
yoke, yolk; awoke, baroque, bespoke, con-
voke, evoke, invoke, provoke, revoke; arti-
choke, counterstroke, gentlefolk, master-
stroke, Roanoke.

-okes. See **-oax.**

-ol (-ŏl), doll, loll, moll, Sol; atoll; alcohol,
capitol, folderol, parasol, protocol, vitriol;
cholesterol.

-ol (-ōl). See **-ole.**

-old, bold, cold, fold, gold, hold, mold,
mould, old, scold, sold, told, wold; behold,
blindfold, cuckold, enfold, foothold, fore-
told, freehold, household, retold, strong-
hold, threshold, toehold, twofold, unfold,
untold, uphold, withhold; centerfold, mani-
fold, marigold, overbold.
Also: **-oal** + **-ed** (as in *foaled,* etc.)
Also: **-ole** + **-ed** (as in *paroled,* etc.)
Also: **-oll** + **-ed** (as in *rolled,* etc.)

-ole, bole, boll, bowl, coal, dole, droll, foal,
goal, hole, Joel, knoll, kohl, mole, pole,
poll, role, roll, scroll, shoal, skoal, sole,
soul, stole, stroll, thole, toll, troll, whole;

bankroll, cajole, condole, console, control, Creole, enroll, flagpole, loophole, Maypole, Nicole, parole, patrol, payroll, peephole, petrol; aerosol, Anatole, barcarole, buttonhole, camisole, girandole, girasole, oriole, rigmarole, rock 'n' roll, Seminole; fillet of sole.

-oled. See **-old.**

-olk. See **-oke.**

-oll (-ol). See **-ol.**

-oll (-ōl). See **-ole.**

-olled. See **-old.**

-olt, bolt, colt, dolt, holt, jolt, molt, poult, volt; revolt, unbolt; thunderbolt.

-olve, solve; absolve, convolve, devolve, dissolve, evolve, involve, resolve, revolve.

-om (-om), bomb, dom, from, prom, rhomb, ROM, Tom; aplomb, pogrom, pompom, therefrom, wherefrom.

-om (-ōōm). See **-oom.**

-omb (-om). See **-om.**

-omb (-ōm). See **-om.**

-omb (-ōōm). See **-oom.**

-ome (-ōm), chrome, comb, dome, foam, gnome, holm, home, loam, mome, Nome, ohm, roam, Rome, tome; cockscomb, coulomb, Jerome, syndrome; aerodrome, catacomb, currycomb, gastronome, hippodrome, honeycomb, metronome, monochrome, palindrome, ribosome, Styrofoam.

-ome (-um). See **-um.**

-omp, comp, pomp, romp, swamp.

-ompt, prompt, romped, swamped.

-on (-ôn), awn, bawn, brawn, dawn, drawn,

faun, fawn, gone, lawn, pawn, prawn,
sawn, Sean, spawn, yawn; begone, bygone, hands-on, head-on, hereon, indrawn,
odds-on, thereon, turned-on, upon,
walk-on, whereon, withdrawn; goings-on,
hanger-on, hereupon, putupon, thereupon,
whereupon, woebegone.

-on (-on), con, don, gone, John, on, scone,
swan, wan, yon; anon, Argonne, Aswan,
begone, bonbon, bygone, Ceylon, chiffon,
cretonne, hereon, icon, neutron, proton,
teflon, thereon, upon, Yvonne; Algernon,
Amazon, antiphon, Aragon, Avalon, beta-
tron, bevatron, colophon, decagon, deu-
teron, echelon, electron, epsilon, Helicon,
hexagon, lexicon, Marathon, marathon,
mastodon, mesotron, myrmidon, nonagon,
Oberon, octagon, omicron, Oregon, para-
gon, Parmesan, Parthenon, Pentagon, poly-
gon, Rubicon, silicon, synchrotron, tarra-
gon, upsilon; Agamemnon, phenomenon,
Saskatchewan; prolegomenon.

-on (-un). See **-un.**

-once (-ons), Hans, nonce, sconce, wants;
ensconce, response.
   Also: **-aunt** + **-s** (as in *taunts,* etc.)

-once (-uns). See **-unce.**

-onch. See **-onk.**

-ond, blond, blonde, bond, fond, frond,
pond, wand, yond; abscond, beyond, de-
spond, respond; correspond, demimonde,
vagabond.
   Also: **-on** + **-ed** (as in *donned,* etc.)

-one (-ōn), bone, blown, cone, crone, drone,
flown, groan, grown, hone, Joan, known,

loan, lone, moan, mohn, mown, own,
phone, pone, prone, roan, Rhone, scone,
shone, shown, sown, stone, throne,
thrown, tone, zone; alone, atone, back-
bone, Bayonne, bemoan, brimstone, cell-
phone, cologne, Cologne, condone, curb-
stone, dethrone, disown, enthrone,
flagstone, grindstone, headstone, intone,
keystone, milestone, millstone, moonstone,
ozone, postpone, trombone, unknown, un-
sewn; baritone, chaperone, cicerone, cor-
nerstone, gramaphone, megaphone, micro-
phone, monotone, overgrown, overthrown,
saxophone, speakerphone, telephone, un-
dertone, xylophone; testosterone.

-one (-on). See **-on.**

-one (-un). See **-un.**

-ong (-ong), gong, long, prong, song, strong,
thong, throng, tong, Tong, wrong; along,
belong, chaise longue, dingdong, diph-
thong, dugong, headlong, headstrong,
Hong Kong, King Kong, lifelong, mah-
jongg, oblong, pingpong, prolong, sidelong,
souchong; evensong, overlong.

-ong (-ung). See **-ung.**

-ongue. See **-ung.**

-onk (-onk), conch, conk, honk; Poulenc;
honky-tonk.

-onk (-unk). See **-unk.**

-onned. See **-ond.**

-onse. See **-once.**

-ont (-ont), font, want; Piedmont, Vermont;
Hellespont.

-ont (-unt). See **-unt.**

-oo. See **-ew.**

-ood (-ŏŏd), could, good, hood, should, stood, wood, would; childhood, firewood, manhood, monkshood, withstood; baby-hood, brotherhood, fatherhood, hardihood, Hollywood, likelihood, livelihood, maiden-hood, motherhood, neighborhood, parent-hood, Robin Hood, sandalwood, sister-hood, understood, womanhood; misunderstood.

-ood (-ōōd). See **-ude.**

-oof, goof, hoof, pouf, proof, roof, spoof, woof; aloof, behoof, disproof, fireproof, rainproof, reproof, Tartuffe; waterproof, weatherproof; opera bouffe.

-ook (-ŏŏk), book, brook, cook, crook, hook, look, nook, rook, shook, took; betook, Chi-nook, forsook, mistook, nainsook, outlook, partook; overlook, pocketbook, undertook.

-ook (-ook). See **-uke.**

-ool, cool, drool, fool, ghoul, pool, rule, school, spool, stool, tool, tulle, who'll; am-poule, befool, footstool, home rule, mis-rule, toadstool, whirlpool; Istanbul, Liver-pool, overrule. See also **-ule.**

-oom, bloom, boom, broom, brume, doom, flume, fume, gloom, groom, loom, plume, rheum, room, spume, tomb, whom, womb; abloom, assume, bridegroom, con-sume, costume, entomb, exhume, Fiume, heirloom, illume, Khartoum, legume, per-fume, presume, relume, resume, simoom, subsume; anteroom, elbowroom, heca-tomb, reassume.

-oon, boon, Boone, coon, croon, dune, goon, hewn, June, loon, moon, noon, prune,

rune, soon, spoon, swoon, tune; attune, baboon, balloon, bassoon, bestrewn, buffoon, cartoon, cocoon, commune, doubloon, dragoon, festoon, forenoon, galloon, harpoon, high noon, immune, impugn, jejune, lagoon, lampoon, maroon, monsoon, oppugn, platoon, poltroon, pontoon, quadroon, raccoon, Rangoon, Simoon, spittoon, tycoon, typhoon, Walloon; afternoon, Brigadoon, Cameroon, honeymoon, importune, macaroon, octoroon, opportune, pantaloon, picaroon, picayune, rigadoon.

-ooned. See **-ound.**

-oop, coop, croup, droop, drupe, dupe, goop, group, hoop, jupe, loop, poop, scoop, sloop, soup, stoop, stoup, stupe, swoop, troop, troupe, whoop; recoup; Guadeloupe, nincompoop.

-oor (-o͞or), boor, brewer, dour, moor, poor, Ruhr, sewer, spoor, sure, tour, Ur; abjure, adjure, amour, assure, brochure, contour, detour, ensure, insure, tonsure, unsure; blackamoor, cynosure, Kohinoor, paramour, petit four, reassure, troubadour; affaire d'amour. See also **-ure.**

-oor (-ôr). See **-ore.**

-oors. See **-ours.**

-oose (-o͞os), Bruce, deuce, goose, juice, loose, moose, mousse, noose, puce, sluice, spruce, truce, use, Zeus; abduce, abstruse, abuse, adduce, burnoose, caboose, conduce, couscous, deduce, diffuse, disuse, excuse, induce, misuse, mongoose, obtuse, papoose, produce, profuse, recluse, reduce, seduce, soukous, Toulouse, traduce, va-

moose; calaboose, charlotte russe, intro-
duce, reproduce, Syracuse; hypotenuse.

-oose (-o͞oz). See **-ooze.**

-oosed. See **-oost.**

-oost, boost, deuced, Proust, roost.
Also: **-uce** + **-ed** (as in *reduced*, etc.)
Also: **-oose** + **-ed** (as in *loosed*, etc.)

-oot (-o͞ot). See **-ute.**

-oot (-o͝ot), foot, put, soot; afoot, forefoot,
hotfoot, input, output; pussyfoot, tender-
foot, underfoot.

-ooth (-o͞oth), booth, couth, ruth, Ruth,
sleuth, sooth, tooth, truth, youth; Duluth,
forsooth, uncouth, vermouth.

-oothe (-o͞oth), smooth, soothe.

-oove. See **-ove.**

-ooze. See **-use.**

-op, bop, chop, cop, crop, drop, flop, fop,
hop, lop, mop, plop, pop, prop, shop, slop,
sop, stop, strop, swap, top; Aesop, atop,
co-op, dewdrop, eavesdrop, estop, flipflop,
snowdrop, tiptop, workshop; aftercrop, lol-
lipop, Malaprop, overstop, whistle-stop.

-ope, cope, dope, grope, hope, lope, mope,
nope, ope, pope, rope, scope, slope, soap,
taupe, tope, trope; elope; antelope, anti-
pope, cantaloupe, envelope, gyroscope,
horoscope, interlope, isotope, microscope,
misanthrope, periscope, stethoscope, tele-
scope; heliotrope, kaleidoscope.

-opped. See **-opt.**

-opt, copt, opt; adopt.
Also: **-op** + **-ed** (as in *topped*, etc.)

-or (-ôr), for, lor, nor, or, Thor, tor, war; ab-
hor, bailor, Dior, donor, furor, junior, les-

sor, senior, vendor; ancestor, auditor, bachelor, chancellor, conqueror, corridor, creditor, counselor, cuspidor, dinosaur, Ecuador, editor, emperor, governor, guarantor, janitor, Labrador, matador, metaphor, meteor, minotaur, monitor, orator, picador, Salvador, senator, troubadour, visitor, warrior; ambassador, competitor, compositor, conspirator, contributor, depositor, executor, ichthyosaur, inheritor, inquisitor, progenitor, proprietor, solicitor, toreador, tyrannosaur. See also **-ore.**

-or (-ər), bailor, donor, furor, junior, senior, vendor; ancestor, auditor, bachelor, chancellor, conqueror, creditor, counselor, editor, emperor, governor, janitor, senator, visitor, warrior; ambassador, competitor, compositor, conspirator, contributor, depositor, executor, inheritor, inquisitor, progenitor, proprietor, solicitor. See also **-ore.**

-or (-ōr). See **-ore.**

-orb, orb; absorb.

-orce. See **-orse.**

-orch, porch, scorch, torch.

-ord, board, chord, cord, fjord, ford, Ford, gourd, hoard, horde, lord, sward, sword, toward, ward; aboard, abhorred, accord, afford, award, broadsword, concord, discord, landlord, record, reward, seaboard, untoward; clavichord, harpsichord, mortarboard, smorgasbord, storyboard; misericord, particleboard.

    Also: **-oar** + **-ed** (as in *roared,* etc.)
    Also: **-ore** + **-ed** (as in *scored,* etc.)

-ore (-ôr) *or* (-ōr), boar, Boer, bore, chore,

core, corps, door, floor, fore, frore, four,
gore, hoar, lore, more, oar, o'er, ore, pore,
pour, roar, score, shore, snore, soar, sore,
store, swore, tore, whore, wore, yore;
adore, afore, ashore, before, claymore, de-
plore, encore, explore, folklore, footsore,
forbore, forswore, galore, heartsore, ig-
nore, implore, restore, señor; albacore, bat-
tledore, Baltimore, commodore, evermore,
furthermore, hellebore, heretofore, never-
more, pinafore, sagamore, semaphore, Sin-
gapore, sophomore, stevedore, sycamore,
underscore. See also **-or.**

-ored. See **-ord.**

-orf, corf, dwarf, Orff, wharf; endomorph,
mesomorph, perimorph.

-orge, forge, George, gorge; disgorge, en-
gorge, regorge.

-ork, cork, Cork, fork, pork, stork, torque,
York; bulwark, New York, pitchfork, un-
cork.

-orld, whorled, world; old-world; nether-
world, otherworld, underworld.
     Also: **-url** + **-ed** (as in *curled*, etc.)

-orm, corm, dorm, form, norm, storm,
swarm, warm; brainstorm, conform, de-
form, inform, misform, perform, reform,
snowstorm, transform; chloroform, cruci-
form, misinform, multiform, thunderstorm,
uniform, vermiform; cuneiform, iodoform.

-orn, born, borne, bourn, corn, horn, lorn,
morn, mourn, scorn, shorn, sworn, thorn,
torn, warn, worn; acorn, adorn, black-
thorn, buckthorn, first-born, foghorn, fore-
warn, forlorn, forsworn, greenhorn, haw-

thorn, Leghorn, lovelorn, outworn, popcorn, stillborn, suborn, toilworn, unborn; alpenhorn, barleycorn, Capricorn, Matterhorn, peppercorn, unicorn, yestermorn.

-orp, dorp, thorp, warp.

-orse, coarse, corse, course, force, gorse, hoarse, horse, Morse, Norse, source, torse; concourse, discourse, divorce, endorse, enforce, perforce, recourse, remorse, resource, seahorse, unhorse; hobbyhorse, intercourse, reinforce, watercourse.

-orst. See **-urst.**

-ort, bort, court, fort, forte, mort, ort, port, quart, short, snort, sort, sport, swart, thwart, tort, torte, wart; abort, airport, assort, athwart, cavort, cohort, comport, consort, contort, deport, disport, distort, escort, exhort, export, extort, import, Newport, passport, purport, rapport, report, resort, retort, seaport, Shreveport, transport; Saint John's wort.

-orth, forth, fourth, north, swarth; henceforth, thenceforth.

-orts, courts, quartz, shorts, sports.

-ose (-ōs), close, dose, gross; cosmos, dextrose, engross, globose, glucose, jocose, lactose, morose, verbose; acerose, adios, adipose, bellicose, cellulose, comatose, diagnose, grandiose, lachrymose, otiose, overdose.

-ose (-ōz), chose, close, clothes, doze, froze, gloze, hose, nose, pose, prose, rose, Rose, those; Ambrose, arose, compose, depose, disclose, dispose, enclose, expose, foreclose, impose, inclose, oppose, propose, repose, suppose, transpose, unclose, unfroze; decompose, discompose, indispose, interpose, predispose, presuppose, tuberose, twinkle-toes; metamorphose, superimpose.

  Also: **-o** + **-s** (as in *punctilios,* etc.)
  Also: **-o** + **-es** (as in *goes,* etc.)
  Also: **-oe** + **-s** (as in *toes,* etc.)
  Also: **-ot** + **-s** (as in *depots,* etc.)
  Also: **-ow** + **-s** (as in *glows,* etc.)

-osh. See **-ash.**

-osk, bosk, mosque; kiosk.

-osque. See **-osk.**

-oss, boss, cos, cross, dross, floss, fosse, gloss, hoss, joss, loss, moss, os, Ross, sauce, toss; across, cosmos, emboss, Eros, lacrosse; albatross, applesauce, reredos, Thanatos; rhinoceros.

-ost (-ôst or -ost), cost, frost, lost, wast; accost, exhaust; holocaust, Pentecost, permafrost.

  Also: **-oss** + **-ed** (as in *tossed,* etc.)

-ost (-ōst), boast, coast, ghost, grossed, host, most, oast, post, roast, toast; almost, engrossed, foremost, hindmost, riposte, seacoast, signpost; aftermost, furthermost, hindermost, hitching post, innermost, lowermost, nethermost, outermost, undermost, uppermost.

-ot, blot, clot, cot, dot, Dot, got, grot, hot, jot, knot, lot, not, plot, pot, rot, scot, Scot, shot, slot, snot, sot, spot, squat, tot, trot, watt, what, wot, yacht; allot, begot, besot, bloodshot, boycott, cocotte, Crockpot, culotte, dogtrot, ergot, forgot, foxtrot, fylfot,

garotte, gavotte, grapeshot, kumquat, lo-
quat, somewhat, unknot; Aldershot, ali-
quot, apricot, bergamot, Camelot, caveat,
counterplot, diddley-squat, eschalot, galli-
pot, Hottentot, Huguenot, Lancelot, misbe-
got, ocelot, patriot, Penobscot, polyglot,
sans-culotte, tommyrot, unbegot, under-
shot; forget-me-not.
    See also **-ought.**

-otch, blotch, botch, crotch, notch, scotch,
Scotch, splotch, swatch, watch; death-
watch, debauch, hopscotch, hotchpotch,
stopwatch, topnotch.

-ote, bloat, boat, Choate, coat, cote, dote,
float, gloat, goat, groat, moat, mote, note,
oat, quote, rote, shoat, smote, stoat,
throat, tote, vote, wrote; afloat, capote,
catboat, compote, connote, coyote, de-
mote, denote, devote, emote, footnote,
keynote, lifeboat, misquote, outvote, pro-
mote, remote, steamboat, topcoat, un-
quote; anecdote, antidote, asymptote, billy-
goat, creosote, nanny goat, overcoat,
petticoat, redingote, riverboat, sugarcoat,
table d'hôte; witenagemot.

-oth (-ôth), broth, cloth, froth, Goth, moth,
swath, Thoth, troth, wroth; betroth, broad-
cloth, sackcloth; Ashtaroth, behemoth, Os-
trogoth, Visigoth.

-oth (-ōth), both, growth, loath, oath, quoth,
sloth, wroth; overgrowth, undergrowth.

-othe (-ōth), clothe, loathe; betroth.

-ou (-ou). See **-ow.**

-ou (-yo͞o). See **-ew.**

-oubt. See **-out.**

-ouch (-ouch), couch, crouch, grouch, ouch, pouch, slouch, vouch; avouch.

-ouch (-uch). See **-utch.**

-ouche (-ōōsh), douche, louche, ruche, whoosh; barouche, cartouche, debouch; scaramouch.

-oud, cloud, crowd, loud, proud, shroud; aloud, becloud, enshroud, o'ercloud; overcloud, overcrowd, thundercloud.

    Also: **-ow** + **-ed** (as in *bowed,* etc.)

-ough (-ôf). See **-off.**

-ough (-ou or -ō). See **-ow.**

-ough (-uf). See **-uff.**

-oughed. See **-oft.**

-ought, aught, bought, brought, caught, fought, fraught, naught, nought, ought, sought, taught, taut, thought, wrought; besought, Connaught, distraught, dreadnought, forethought, methought, onslaught; aeronaut, afterthought, Argonaut, astronaut, cosmonaut, juggernaut, overwrought.

    See also **-ot.**

-oul (-oul). See **-owl.**

-oul (-ōl). See **-ole.**

-ould. See **-ood.**

-oun. See **-own.**

-ounce, bounce, flounce, frounce, jounce, ounce, pounce, trounce; announce, denounce, enounce, pronounce, renounce.

    Also: **-ount** + **-s** (as in *counts,* etc.)

-ound (-ound), bound, found, ground, hound, mound, pound, round, sound, wound; abound, aground, around, astound, background, bloodhound, compound, confound, dumfound, expound, hidebound, homebound, horehound, icebound, inbound, outbound, profound, propound, rebound, redound, resound, spellbound, snowbound, surround, unbound, unfound; ultrasound, underground, wraparound; merry-go-round.

Also: **-own** + **-ed** (as in *clowned*, etc.)

-ound (-ōōnd), wound.

Also: **-oon** + **-ed** (as in *swooned*, etc.)
Also: **-une** + **-ed** (as in *tuned*, etc.)

-ount, count, fount, mount; account, amount, discount, dismount, miscount, recount, remount, surmount, viscount; catamount, paramount, tantamount.

-ounts. See **-ounce.**

-oup. See **-oop.**

-our, bower, cower, dour, dower, flour, flower, glower, hour, lour, lower, our, power, scour, shower, sour, tower; deflower, devour, embower, empower, horsepower, manpower, sunflower, wallflower; Adenauer, cauliflower, Eisenhower, overpower.

Also: **-ow** + **-er** (as in *plower*, etc.)

-ourge. See **-erge.**

-ourn (-ôrn). See **-orn.**

-ourn (-ûrn). See **-urn.**

-ours (-ourz), ours.

Also: **-our** + **-s** (as in *devours*, etc.)
Also: **-ower** + **-s** (as in *flowers*, etc.)

-ours (-ōōrz), yours.

Also: **-oor** + **-s** (as in *boors*, etc.)
Also: **-our** + **-s** (as in *amours*, etc.)
Also: **-ure** + **-s** (as in *lures*, etc.)

-ourse. See **-orse.**

-ourt. See **-ort.**

-ourth. See **-orth.**

-ous. See **-us.**

-ouse, blouse, douse, grouse, house, louse, mouse, souse, spouse, Strauss; backhouse, Bauhaus, birdhouse, clubhouse, delouse, doghouse, hothouse, jailhouse, lighthouse, madhouse, outhouse, penthouse, poorhouse, roundhouse, storehouse, warehouse, workhouse; Fledermaus, Mickey Mouse, powerhouse, summerhouse.

-oust, doused, Faust, joust, oust, soused, spoused; deloused.

-out, bout, clout, doubt, drought, flout, gout, grout, knout, kraut, lout, out, pout, rout, scout, shout, snout, spout, sprout, stout, tout, trout; ablaut, about, blackout, brownout, devout, lookout, redoubt, takeout, throughout, umlaut, whiteout, without; gadabout, hereabout, knockabout, out-and-out, roundabout, roustabout, sauerkraut, thereabout, waterspout, whereabout.

-outh (-outh), drouth, mouth, south.

-outh (-ōōth). See **-ooth.**

-ove (-uv), dove, glove, love, of, shove; above, foxglove, hereof, thereof, unglove, whereof; ladylove, turtledove.

-ove (-ōv), clove, cove, dove, drove, grove, hove, Jove, mauve, rove, shrove, stove, strove, throve, trove, wove; alcove, mangrove; borogrove, interwove, treasure trove.

-ove (-ōōv), groove, move, prove, who've,

you've; approve, behoove, disprove, improve, remove, reprove; disapprove.

-ow (-ou), bough, bow, brow, chow, ciao, cow, dhow, Dow, frau, how, now, plough, plow, prow, row, scow, slough, sow, Tao, tau, thou, vow, wow; allow, avow, bowwow, endow, enow, highbrow, hoosegow, know-how, kowtow, landau, lowbrow, Mau Mau, meow, Moldau, Moscow, powwow, snowplow, somehow, anyhow, disallow, disavow, middlebrow; Oberammergau.

-ow (-ō), beau, blow, bow, crow, do, doe, dough, eau, Flo, floe, flow, foe, fro, glow, go, grow, hoe, Jo, Joe, know, lo, low, mot, mow, no, O, oh, owe, Po, pro, rho, roe, row, sew, show, sloe, slow, snow, so, sow, stow, Stowe, strow, throe, throw, toe, tow, trow, whoa, woe, Zoe; aglow, ago, although, banjo, below, bestow, bon mot, Bordeaux, bravo, bubo, bureau, chapeau, château, Chi-Rho, cockcrow, cocoa, dado, Defoe, depot, dido, Dido, duo, euro, forego, foreknow, foreshow, Frisco, heigh-ho, hello, jabot, Jane Doe, John Doe, Keogh, KO, macho, Marlow, merlot, Miró, Monroe, moonglow, no-show, nouveau, oboe, outgrow, Pernod, Perot, pierrot, Pinot, poncho, quarto, rainbow, rondeau, Rousseau, sabot, tableau, tiptoe, toro, trousseau, van Gogh, Watteau, zero; ab ovo, afterglow, albedo, al fresco, allegro, apropos, buffalo, Buffalo, bungalow, calico, cameo, Cicero, Diderot, domino, embryo, Eskimo, falsetto, Figaro, folio, furbelow, gazebo, gigolo, HMO, Iago, Idaho,

indigo, Mario, memento, Mexico, mistle-
toe, mulatto, memento, Mexico, nuncio, octavo, Ohio,
oleo, overflow, overgrow, overthrow, por-
tico, portmanteau, potato, Prospero, prox-
imo, radio, Romeo, sloppy joe, so-and-so,
sourdough, stiletto, studio, tae kwon do,
tallyho, tobacco, Tokyo, tomato, torero,
torpedo, tremolo, ultimo, undergo, under-
tow, vertigo, video, vireo, volcano; Abed-
nego, Acapulco, adagio, bravissimo, ex ni-
hilo, fortissimo, imbroglio, incognito,
intaglio, magnifico, malapropos, musta-
chio, Ontario, oregano, pistachio, politico,
seraglio; ab initio, archipelago, banderillero, braggadoccio, duodecimo, ex officio,
impresario, oratorio, pianissimo; generalis-
simo.

-owd. See **-oud.**

-owed (-ōd). See **-ode.**

-owed (-oud). See **-oud.**

-ower. See **-our.**

-owl, cowl, foul, fowl, growl, howl, jowl,
owl, prowl, scowl, yowl; befoul, water-
fowl.

-own (-oun), brown, Brown,clown, crown,
down, drown, frown, gown, noun, town;
adown, boomtown, Capetown, downtown,
embrown, Georgetown, Jamestown, night-
gown, pronoun, renown, uptown; Allen-
town, buttondown, Chinatown, eiderdown,
hand-me-down, shantytown, tumble-down,
upside down, watered-down.

-own (-ōn). See **-one.**

-owned. See **-ound.**

-ows (-ōz). See **-ose.**

-ows (-ouz). See **-owse**.

-owse, blowse, browse, dowse, drowse,
house, rouse, spouse; arouse, carouse, es-
pouse.
    Also: **-ow** + **-s** (as in *cows,* etc.)

-owth. See **-oth**.

-ox, box, cox, fox, lox, ox, phlox, pox, sox,
vox; bandbox, hatbox, icebox, mailbox,
postbox, smallpox, soapbox, Xerox; chick-
enpox, equinox, orthodox, paradox; hetero-
dox.
    Also: **-ock** + **-s** (as in *knocks,* etc.)

-oy, boy, buoy, cloy, coy, goy, joy, oy, ploy,
poi, Roy, soy, toy, troy, Troy; ahoy, alloy,
annoy, batboy, bok choy, busboy, choir-
boy, convoy, decoy, deploy, destroy, employ, enjoy, envoy, Leroy, McCoy, Rob
Roy, Saint Croix, Savoy, sepoy, viceroy;
corduroy, hoi polloi, Illinois, Iroquois, mis-
employ, overjoy, Tinkertoy; hobbledehoy.

-oyed. See **-oid**.

-oys. See **-oise**.

-oze. See **-ose**.

-ub, bub, chub, club, cub, drub, dub, grub,
hub, nub, pub, rub, scrub, shrub, snub,
stub, sub, tub; hubbub; rub-a-dub, silla-
bub; Beelzebub.

-ube, boob, cube, rube, Rube, tube; jujube.

-uce. See **-oose**.

-uced. See **-oost**.

-uch. See **-utch**.

-uck, buck, chuck, cluck, duck, luck, muck,
pluck, puck, Puck, ruck, schmuck, shuck,
snuck, struck, stuck, suck, truck, tuck;
amok, amuck, awestruck, dumbstruck,

lameduck, moonstruck, potluck, roebuck, stagestruck, starstruck, woodchuck; Habakkuk, horror-struck, terror-struck, thunderstruck, wonderstruck.

-ucked. See **-uct.**

-ucks. See **-ux.**

-uct, duct; abduct, conduct, construct, deduct, induct, instruct, obstruct; aqueduct, misconduct, oviduct, usufruct, viaduct.

Also: **-uck** + **-ed** (as in *tucked,* etc.)

-ud, blood, bud, cud, dud, flood, mud, scud, spud, stud, sud, thud; bestud, lifeblood, rosebud.

-ude, brood, crude, dude, feud, food, Jude, lewd, mood, nude, prude, rood, rude, shrewd, snood, you'd, who'd; allude, collude, conclude, delude, denude, elude, étude, exclude, extrude, exude, include, intrude, obtrude, occlude, preclude, prelude, protrude, seclude; altitude, amplitude, aptitude, certitude, desuetude, fortitude, gratitude, habitude, interlude, lassitude, latitude, longitude, magnitude, multitude, platitude, plenitude, promptitude, pulchritude, quietude, rectitude, servitude, solitude, turpitude; beatitude, exactitude, ingratitude, necessitude, similitude, solicitude, vicissitude, verisimilitude.

Also: **-ew** + **-ed** (as in *brewed,* etc.)
Also: **-oo** + **-ed** (as in *wooed,* etc.)
Also: **-ue** + **-ed** (as in *pursued,* etc.)

-udge, budge, drudge, fudge, grudge, judge, nudge, sludge, smudge, trudge; adjudge, begrudge, forejudge, misjudge, prejudge.

-ue. See **-ew.**

-ues. See **-ooze** and **-use.**

-uff, bluff, buff, chough, chuff, cuff, duff, fluff, gruff, guff, huff, luff, muff, puff, rough, ruff, scruff, scuff, slough, snuff, sough, stuff, tough, tuff; breadstuff, earmuff, enough, Macduff, rebuff; overstuff, powderpuff.

-ug, bug, chug, drug, dug, hug, jug, lug, mug, plug, pug, rug, shrug, slug, smug, snug, thug, tug; humbug; doodlebug, jitterbug, litterbug, mealybug.

-uge, huge, luge, Scrooge, stooge; deluge; refuge; centrifuge, febrifuge, subterfuge, vermifuge.

-uice. See **-oose.**

-uise. See **-ize.**

-uke, cuke, duke, fluke, Juke, Luke, nuke, puke, snook, spook, uke; archduke, Baruch, caoutchouc, Chinook, peruke, rebuke; Heptateuch, Mameluke, Marmaduke, Pentateuch.

-ul (-ul), cull, dull, gull, hull, lull, mull, null, scull, skull, trull; annul, mogul, numskull, seagull.

-ul (-ool), bull, full, pull, wool; cupful, graceful, lambswool; beautiful, bountiful, dutiful, fanciful, masterful, merciful, pitiful, plentiful, powerful, Sitting Bull, sorrowful, teaspoonful, wonderful, worshipful; tablespoonful.

-ulch, culch, gulch, mulch.

-ule, fuel, mewl, mule, pule, you'll, yule; ampule; molecule, reticule, ridicule, vestibule. See also **-ool.**

-ulge, bulge; divulge, effulge, indulge.

-ulk, bulk, hulk, skulk, sulk.

-ull. See **-ul.**

-ulp, gulp, pulp, sculp.

-ulse, pulse; convulse, impulse, repulse.

-ult, cult; adult, consult, exult, insult, occult, result, tumult; catapult, difficult; antepenult.

-um, bum, chum, come, crumb, drum, dumb, glum, grum, gum, hum, mum, numb, plum, plumb, rum, scum, slum, some, strum, stum, sum, swum, thrum, thumb; become, benumb, humdrum, pablum, spectrum, succumb; burdensome, Christendom, cranium, cumbersome, frolicsome, heathendom, kettledrum, laudanum, martyrdom, maximum, medium, mettlesome, minimum, modicum, odium, opium, optimum, overcome, pendulum, platinum, podium, premium, quarrelsome, quietsome, radium, speculum, sugar plum, tedium, troublesome, tympanum, vacuum, venturesome, wearisome; adventuresome, aluminum, aquarium, chrysanthemum, compendium, continuum, curriculum, delirium, effluvium, emporium, encomium, exordium, fee-fi-fo-fum, geranium, gymnasium, harmonium, magnesium, millennium, opprobrium, palladium, petroleum, residuum, symposium; auditorium, crematorium, equilibrium, pandemonium, sanitarium.

-umb. See **-um.**

-ume. See **-oom.**

-ump, bump, chump, clump, dump, drump, frump, grump, Gump, hump, jump, lump, mump, plump, pump, rump, slump, stump, thump, trump, ump; mugwump.

-un, bun, done, dun, fun, gun, Hun, none, nun, one, pun, run, shun, son, spun, stun, sun, ton, tun, won; begun, homespun, outrun, rerun, someone, undone, Watson; Acheron, Albion, anyone, Chesterton, cinnamon, everyone, galleon, Galveston, garrison, halcyon, hit-and-run, orison, overdone, overrun, simpleton, singleton, skeleton, twenty-one, unison, venison; accordion, comparison, oblivion, phenomenon.

-unce, dunce, once.
   Also: **-unt** + **-s** (as in *bunts*, etc.)

-unch, brunch, bunch, crunch, hunch, lunch, munch, punch, scrunch.

-unct, adjunct, defunct, disjunct.
   Also: **-unk** + **-ed** (as in *bunked*, etc.)

-und, bund, fund; fecund, jocund, obtund, refund, rotund; cummerbund, moribund, orotund, rubicund.
   Also: **-un** + **-ed** (as in *stunned,* etc.)

-une. See **-oon.**

-uned. See **-ound.**

-ung, bung, clung, dung, flung, hung, lung, rung, slung, sprung, strung, stung, sung, swung, tongue, wrung, young; among, highstrung, Shantung, unstrung, unsung; Niebelung, overhung, underslung.

-unge, lunge, plunge, sponge; expunge; muskellunge.

-unk, bunk, chunk, drunk, dunk, flunk, funk, hunk, junk, monk, plunk, punk, shrunk, skunk, slunk, spunk, sunk, trunk;

adunc, kerplunk, Podunk, punchdrunk, quidnunc, spelunk.

-unked. See **-unct.**

-unned. See **-und.**

-unt, blunt, brunt, bunt, front, grunt, hunt, punt, runt, shunt, stunt; affront, beach-front, confront, forefront, manhunt, store-front.

-unts. See **-unce.**

-up, cup, pup, sup, tup, up; backup, bang-up, blowup, built-up, catch-up, checkup, eggcup, fill-up, foul-up, grown-up, hiccup, makeup, mock-up, setup, sit-up, slipup, teacup, thumbs-up, tossup, touchup, trumped-up, tune-up, washed-up, windup; buttercup, cover-up, higher-up, pick-me-up, runner-up; Johnny-jump-up, sunny-side up.

-upe. See **-oop.**

-upt, abrupt, corrupt, disrupt, erupt; inter-rupt.

Also: **-up** + **-ed** (as in *supped,* etc.)

-ur. See **-er.**

-urb. See **-erb.**

-urch, birch, church, lurch, perch, search, smirch; besmirch, research.

-urd, bird, curd, gird, heard, herd, Kurd, nerd, surd, third, word; absurd, blackbird, lovebird, songbird, ungird, unheard; hum-mingbird, ladybird, mockingbird, over-heard.

Also: **-er** + **-ed** (as in *conferred,* etc.)
Also: **-ir** + **-ed** (as in *stirred,* etc.)
Also: **-ur** + **-ed** (as in *occurred,* etc.)

-ure, cure, lure, pure, your, you're; allure,

assure, cocksure, coiffure, demure, endure,
immure, impure, inure, manure, mature,
obscure, ordure, procure, secure; amateur,
aperture, armature, epicure, forfeiture, fur-
niture, immature, insecure, ligature, over-
ture, portraiture, premature, reassure, sig-
nature, sinecure; caricature, expenditure,
investiture, literature, miniature, muscula-
ture, nomenclature, temperature; primo-
geniture. See also **-oor.**

-ures. See **-ours.**

-urf, scurf, serf, surf, turf.

-urge. See **-erge.**

-urk, burke, Burke, cirque, clerk, dirk, Dirk,
irk, jerk, kirk, Kirk,lurk, murk, perk, quirk,
shirk, smirk, Turk, work; artwork, berserk,
bridgework, Dunkirk, guesswork, home-
work, housework, rework; busywork,
handiwork, masterwork, overwork, soda
jerk, underwork.

-url, Beryl, burl, churl, curl, earl, furl, girl,
hurl, knurl, pearl, purl, swirl, twirl, whirl,
whorl; uncurl, unfurl.

-urled. See **-orld.**

-urn, Berne, burn, churn, earn, erne, fern,
hern, kern, learn, quern, spurn, stern, tern,
turn, urn, yearn; adjourn, astern, concern,
discern, eterne, intern, Lucerne, nocturne,
return, sojourn, unlearn; overturn, taci-
turn, unconcern.

-urp, burp, chirp, slurp, stirp, twerp; usurp.

-urred. See **-urd.**

-urse. See **-erse.**

-ursed. See **-urst.**

-urst, burst, curst, durst, erst, first, Hearst,

thirst, verst, worst; accurst, athirst, knack-
wurst, outburst, sunburst; liverwurst.

Also: **-erce** + **-ed** (as in *coerced,* etc.)

Also: **-erse** + **-ed** (as in *dispersed,* etc.)

Also: **-urse** + **-ed** (as in *nursed,* etc.)

-urve. See **-erve.**

-us, bus, buss, cuss, fuss, Gus, Hus, muss,
plus, pus, Russ, thus, truss, us; cirrus, dis-
cuss, nimbus, nonplus, percuss, Remus,
stratus; abacus, Angelus, animus, blunder-
buss, cumulus, exodus, Hesperus, impetus,
incubus, minibus, nautilus, octopus, Oedi-
pus, omnibus, Pegasus, platypus, Priapus,
radius, Romulus, Sirius, stimulus, succu-
bus, Tantalus, terminus; esophagus, Ho-
munculus, Leviticus, sarcophagus.

Also: numerous words ending in **-ous**
(as *mutinous, perilous,* etc.)

-use (-yōoz), blues, booze, bruise, Druze,
fuse, fuze, lose, mews, muse, news, ooze,
ruse, shoes, snooze, use, who's, whose;
abuse, accuse, amuse, bemuse, confuse,
diffuse, disuse, enthuse, excuse, infuse,
misuse, peruse, refuse, suffuse, transfuse;
disabuse, Syracuse.

Also: **-ew** + **-s** (as in *stews,* etc.)

Also: **-oo** + **-s** (as in *moos,* etc.)

Also: **-ue** + **-s** (as in *cues,* etc.)

-use (-ōos) or (-yōos). See **-oose.**

-use (-ōoz). See **-ooze.**

-ush (-ush), blush, brush, crush, flush, gush,
hush, lush, mush, plush, rush, shush,
slush, thrush; hairbrush; underbrush.

-ush (-ŏosh), bush, push, shush, squoosh,

swoosh, tush; ambush; bramblebush, Hindu Kush.

-usk, brusque, busk, dusk, husk, musk, rusk, tusk, Usk.

-uss. See **-us.**

-ussed. See **-ust.**

-ust, bust, crust, dost, dust, gust, just, lust, must, rust, thrust, trust; adjust, adust, august, August, combust, disgust, distrust, encrust, entrust, incrust, mistrust, piecrust, robust, stardust, unjust; antitrust, wanderlust.

    Also: **-uss** + **-ed** (as in *fussed*, etc.)

-ut (-ut), but, butt, cut, glut, gut, hut, jut, mutt, nut, putt, rut, shut, slut, smut, strut, tut; abut, beechnut, catgut, chestnut, clearcut, crewcut, haircut, peanut, rebut, rotgut, shortcut, uncut, walnut; betelnut, butternut, coconut, halibut, hazelnut, occiput, scuttlebutt, undercut, uppercut.

-ut (-o͞ot) See **-oot.**

-utch, clutch, crutch, Dutch, hutch, much, smutch, such, touch; retouch; inasmuch, insomuch, overmuch.

-ute, beaut, boot, brute, butte, chute, coot, cute, flute, fruit, hoot, jute, loot, lute, moot, mute, newt, root, route, shoot, skoot, suit, toot, Ute; acute, Aleut, astute, Beirut, breadfruit, cahoot, Canute, cheroot, commute, compute, confute, crapshoot, depute, dilute, dispute, hirsute, impute, minute, Paiute, pollute, pursuit, recruit, refute, repute, salute, transmute, uproot, volute; absolute, attribute, bandicoot, bodysuit, constitute, Denver boot, destitute, disrepute, dissolute, execute, institute, kiwifruit, malamute, overshoot, parachute, persecute, prosecute, prostitute, resolute, substitute; electrocute, Hardecanute, irresolute, reconstitute.

-uth. See **-ooth.**

-ux, crux, flux, lux, shucks, tux; conflux, efflux, influx, reflux; Benelux.

Also: **-uck** + **-s** (as in *plucks*, etc.)

-uzz, buzz, coz, does, fuzz.

-y, ay, aye, buy, by, bye, cry, die, dry, dye, eye, fie, fly, fry, guy, Guy, hi, hie, high, I, lie, lye, my, nigh, phi, pi, pie, ply, pry, psi, rye, shy, sigh, sky, Skye, sly, spry, spy, sty, Thai, thigh, thy, tie, try, vie, why, wry; ally, apply, awry, Bacchae, Baha'i, belie, bone-dry, bonsai, canaille, comply, decry, defy, deny, descry, Eli, espy, GI, goodbye, hereby, imply, knee-high, July, magpie, mudpie, outcry, outvie, popeye, red-eye, rely, reply, sci-fi, semi, Shanghai, shoofly, Sinai, standby, stir fry, supply, thereby, tie-dye, untie, Versailles, whereby; abaci, alibi, alkali, alumni, amplify, beautify, butterfly, by-and-by, certify, citify, clarify, classify, codify, crucify, deify, dignify, edify, falsify, fortify, Gemini, glorify, gratify, horrify, humble pie, hushaby, justify, lazuli, Lorelei, lullaby, magnify, modify, mollify, Mordecai, mortify, multiply, mummify, mystify, notify, nullify, occupy, ossify, pacify, petrify, prophesy, purify, putrefy, qualify, ratify, rectify, sanctify, satisfy, scarify, signify, simplify, specify, stultify, stupefy, terrify, testify, typify, umblepie, unify, verify, versify, vilify; beatify, declassify, demystify, detoxify, Dioscuri, disqualify, diversify, exemplify, humidify, identify, indemnify, intensify, Lotophagi, personify, preoccupy, solemnify, solidify, syllabify, vox populi; Aegospotami, anthropophagi, corpus delicti, modus vivendi; amicus curiae, curriculum vitae, modus operandi.

-yle. See **-ile.**

-yled. See **-ild.**

-yme. See **-ime.**

-ymn. See **-im.**

-ymph, lymph, nymph.

-yne. See **-ine.**

-ynx. See **-inx.**

-yp. See **-ip.**

-ype. See **-ipe.**

-yph. See **-iff.**

-ypse. See **-ipse.**

-yre. See **-ire.**

-yrrh. See **-er.**

-ysm. See **-ism.**

-yst. See **-ist.**

-yte. See **-ite.**

-yth. See **-ith.**

-yve. See **-ive.**

-yx. See **-ix.**

Two-Syllable Rhymes

-abard. See **-abbard.**

-abbard, clapboard, jabbered, scabbard, slabbered, tabard.

-abber (-a-), blabber, clabber, dabber, drabber, grabber, jabber, nabber, slabber, stabber; beslabber.

-abber (-o-). See **-obber.**

-abbered. See **-abbard.**

-abbet. See **-abit.**

-abbey. See **-abby.**

-abbit. See **-abit.**

-abble, babble, dabble, drabble, gabble, grabble, rabble, scabble, scrabble; bedabble, bedrabble, hardscrabble.

-abby, abbey, Abby, cabby, crabby, flabby, Gaby, grabby, scabby, shabby, tabby.

-abel. See **-able.**

-aber. See **-abor.**

-abies, babies, rabies, scabies.

-abit, abbot, babbitt, Babbitt, habit, rabbet, rabbit; cohabit, inhabit, jackrabbit.

-able, Abel, able, babel, cable, fable, gable, label, Mabel, sable, stable, table; disable, enable, timetable, unable, unstable.

-abor, caber, labor, neighbor, saber, tabor, Weber; belabor.

-abra, sabra; candelabra; abracadabra.

-aby, baby, gaby, maybe.

-accy. See **-acky.**

-acement. See **-asement.**

-acence. See **-ascence.**

-acent, jacent, naissant, nascent; adjacent,
complacent, complaisant, connascent, re-
naissant, renascent, subjacent; circumja-
cent, interjacent.

-aceous. See **-acious.**

-acet. See **-asset.**

-achment. See **-atchment.**

-achne. See **-acne.**

-acial, facial, glacial, racial, spatial; abbatial,
palatial, prelatial.

-acic. See **-assic.**

-acid, acid, flaccid, placid.

-acile. See **-astle.**

-acious, gracious, spacious; audacious, bul-
baceous, cactaceous, capacious, cetaceous,
cretaceous, crustaceous, edacious, faba-
ceous, fallacious, feracious, flirtatious, fu-
gacious, fumacious, fungaceous, gemma-
ceous, herbaceous, Horatius, Ignatius,
lappaceous, lardaceous, loquacious, marla-
ceous, mendacious, micaceous, minacious,
misgracious, mordacious, palacious, pal-
maceous, pomaceous, predaceous, proca-
cious, pugnacious, rampacious, rapacious,
rutaceous, sagacious, salacious, sebaceous,
sequacious, setaceous, tenacious, testa-
ceous, tophaceous, ungracious, veracious,
vexatious, vinaceous, vivacious, voracious;
acanaceous, acanthaceous, alliaceous,
amylaceous, arenaceous, camphoraceous,
capillaceous, carbonaceous, contumacious,
corallaceous, coriaceous, disputatious, effi-
cacious, erinaceous, execratious, farina-
ceous, ferulaceous, foliaceous, incapacious,
liliaceous, olivaceous, orchidaceous, osten-

tatious, perspicacious, pertinacious, resinaceous, saponaceous, violaceous; inefficacious.

-acis. See **-asis.**

-acit. See **-asset.**

-acken, blacken, bracken, slacken.

-acker, backer, clacker, cracker, hacker, lacquer, packer, slacker; hijacker, kayaker, nutcracker.

-acket, bracket, flacket, jacket, packet, placket, racket, tacket; straitjacket, yellowjacket.

-ackey. See **-acky.**

-ackguard. See **-aggard.**

-ackie. See **-acky.**

-ackish, blackish, brackish, knackish, quackish.

-ackle, cackle, crackle, hackle, macle, quackle, shackle, spackle, tackle; debacle, ramshackle, unshackle; tabernacle.

-ackney. See **-acne.**

-ackpot, crackpot, jackpot.

-ackson. See **-axen.**

-acky, 'baccy, Jackie, khaki, knacky, lackey, Saki, tacky, wacky; Nagasaki, ticky-tacky.

-acle. See **-ackle.**

-acne, acne, hackney; Arachne.

-acon, bacon, Bacon, Macon. See also **-aken.**

-acquer. See **-acker.**

-acre. See **-aker.**

-acter. See **-actor.**

-actic, lactic, tactic; climactic, didactic, emphractic, galactic, protactic, stalactic, syn-

tactic; parallactic, prophylactic; anticlimactic, intergalactic.
- **-actice,** cactus, practice, malpractice.
- **-actile,** dactyl, tactile, tractile; attractile, contractile, protractile, retractile; pterodactyl.
- **-action,** action, faction, fraction, paction, taction, traction; abstraction, attraction, coaction, compaction, contaction, contraction, detraction, distraction, exaction, extraction, inaction, infraction, protraction, reaction, redaction, refraction, retraction, subaction, subtraction, transaction; arefaction, benefaction, calefaction, counteraction, interaction, labefaction, liquefaction, lubrifaction, malefaction, petrifaction, putrefaction, rarefaction, retroaction, rubefaction, satisfaction, stupefaction, tabefaction, tepefaction, tumefaction; dissatisfaction.
- **-active,** active, tractive; abstractive, attractive, coactive; contractive, detractive, distractive, enactive, inactive, olfactive, protractive, refractive, retractive, subtractive; calefactive, counteractive, petrifactive, putrefactive, retroactive, satisfactive, stupefactive; radioactive.
- **-actly,** abstractly, compactly, exactly; matter-of-factly.
- **-actor,** actor, factor, tractor; abstracter, attracter, climacter, compacter, contractor, detractor, distracter, enacter, exacter, extracter, infractor, olfactor, phylacter, protractor, refractor, retractor, subtracter, transactor; benefactor, malefactor.
- **-acture,** facture, fracture; compacture; manufacture.

-actus. See **-actice.**

-actyl. See **-actile.**

-acy, Casey, lacy, Macy, racy, précis.

-ada, Dada; armada, cicada, Grenada, haggadah, Nevada; autostrada, enchilada; Sierra Nevada.

-adam, Adam, madam; macadam.

-adden, gladden, madden, sadden; Aladdin.

-adder, adder, bladder, gadder, gladder, ladder, madder, padder, sadder; stepladder.

-addie. See **-addy.**

-adding. See **-odding.**

-addish, baddish, caddish, faddish, maddish, radish, saddish.

-addle (-a-), addle, daddle, faddle, paddle, raddle, saddle, staddle, straddle; astraddle, skedaddle, unsaddle; fiddle-faddle.

-addle (-o-). See **-oddle.**

-addock, haddock, paddock, raddock, shaddock.

-addy, caddy, daddy, faddy, haddie, laddie, paddy; finnan-haddie, sugar daddy.

-aden, Aden, laden, maiden.

-ader, aider, grader, raider, seder, trader; crusader, Darth Vader, evader, invader, persuader.

-adger, badger, cadger.

-adi. See **-ady.**

-adiant, gradient, radiant.

-adic, nomadic, sporadic.

-adie. See **-ady.**

-adient. See **-adiant.**

-adish. See **-addish.**

-adle, cradle, dreidel, ladle; encradle.

-adly, badly, gladly, madly, sadly.

-adness, badness, gladness, madness, sadness.

-ado (-ā dō), dado; crusado, gambado, grenado, scalado, stoccado, tornado; ambuscado, barricado, bastinado, camisado, carbonado, desperado, muscovado, renegado.

-ado (-ä dō), bravado, Mikado, passado, strappado, travado; avocado, Colorado, desperado, El Dorado, imbrocado, amontillado; aficionado; incommunicado.

-ady, braidy, cadi, glady, lady, Sadie, shady; belady, cascady, landlady.

-afer, chafer, safer, wafer; cockchafer.

-affer, chaffer, gaffer, Kafir, laugher, zaffer.

-affic. See **-aphic.**

-affick. See **-aphic.**

-affir. See **-affer.**

-affle, baffle, gaffle, haffle, raffle, scraffle, snaffle, yaffle.

-affled, baffled, raffled, scaffold, snaffled.

-affold. See **-affled.**

-affy, baffy, chaffy, daffy, draffy, taffy.

-after, after, dafter, drafter, grafter, hafter, laughter, rafter, wafter; hereafter, ingrafter, thereafter; hereinafter.

-afty, crafty, drafty, grafty.

-agar. See **-agger.**

-agate. See **-aggot.**

-agement, assuagement, encagement, engagement, enragement, presagement.

-ageous, ambagious, contagious, courageous, oragious, outrageous, rampageous, umbrageous; advantageous; disadvantageous.

-ager, cager, gauger, major, pager, sager, stager; assuager, presager.

-aggard, blackguard, haggard, laggard, staggard, staggered, swaggered.

-agger, bragger, dagger, flagger, gagger, jagger, lagger, nagger, ragger, tagger, wagger; agar-agar, carpetbagger.

-aggered. See **-aggard.**

-aggie. See **-aggy.**

-aggish, haggish, naggish, waggish.

-aggle, daggle, draggle, gaggle, haggle, raggle, straggle, waggle; bedaggle, bedraggle; raggle-taggle.

-aggot, agate, faggot, fagot, maggot.

-aggy, Aggie, baggy, craggy, faggy, Maggie, naggy, scraggy, shaggy, slaggy, snaggy, waggy.

-agic, magic, tragic; pelagic; archipelagic.

-agile, agile, fragile.

-agious. See **-ageous.**

-ago (-ā gō), dago, sago; farrago, imago, lumbago, plumbago, virago, vorago.

-ago (-ä gō), Chicago, farrago, virago; Asiago, Santiago.

-agon, dragon, flagon, wagon; bandwagon, pendragon, snapdragon.

-agrant, flagrant, fragrant, vagrant; infragrant.

-aic, laic; Alcaic, altaic, archaic, deltaic, Hebraic, Judaic, mosaic, Mosaic, Passaic, prosaic, sodaic, spondaic, stanzaic, trochaic, voltaic; algebraic, Alhambraic, Aramaic, pharisaic, Ptolemaic, tesseraic; paradisaic.

-aiden. See **-aden.**

-aider. See **-ader.**

-aidy. See **-ady.**

-aighten. See **-atan.**

-aigner. See **-ainer.**

-ailer, ailer, gaoler, jailer, paler, sailor, squalor, staler, tailor, trailer, whaler; blackmailer, retailer, wholesaler.

-ailie. See **-alely.**

-ailiff, bailiff, caliph.

-ailing, ailing, failing, grayling, paling.

-ailment, ailment, bailment; assailment, bewailment, curtailment, derailment, entailment, impalement, regalement.

-ailor. See **-ailer.**

-aily. See **-alely.**

-aiment. See **-ayment.**

-ainder, attainder, remainder.

-ainer, drainer, gainer, plainer, saner, stainer, strainer, trainer; abstainer, attainer, campaigner, chicaner, complainer, container, profaner, retainer; entertainer.

-ainful, baneful, gainful, painful; complainful, disdainful.

-ainger. See **-anger.**

-ainly, gainly, mainly, plainly, sanely, vainly, humanely, inanely, insanely, mundanely, profanely, ungainly, urbanely.

-ainter, fainter, painter, tainter.

-aintly, faintly, quaintly, saintly; unsaintly.

-ainty, dainty, fainty, feinty.

-ainy, brainy, grainy, rainy, veiny, zany; Eugénie; Allegheny, miscellany.

-airie. See **-ary.**

-airing. See **-aring.**
-airish. See **-arish.**
-airly. See **-arely.**
-airy. See **-ary.**
-aisant. See **-acent.**
-aiser. See **-azer.**
-aissant. See **-acent.**
-aisy. See **-azy.**
-aiter. See **-ator.**
-aitress. See **-atress.**
-aiver. See **-aver.**
-ajor. See **-ager.**
-ake. See **-ocky.**
-aken (-ā-), shaken, taken, waken; awaken, forsaken, mistaken; godforsaken. See also **-acon.**
-aker, acre, baker, breaker, faker, fakir, maker, Quaker, raker, shaker, Shaker, taker, waker; bookmaker, dressmaker, grubstaker, heartbreaker, lawbreaker, matchmaker, pacemaker, peacemaker, snowmaker, tiebreaker, watchmaker, windbreaker; boilermaker, circuitbreaker, undertaker.
-aki (-a-). See **-acky.**
-aki (-ä-). See **-ocky.**
-akir. See **-aker.**
-alace. See **-allas.**
-alad, ballad, salad. See also **-alid.**
-alan. See **-allon.**
-alant (-ā-), assailant, covalent, inhalant, surveillant, multivalent.
-alap. See **-allop.**
-alate. See **-allot.**

-aldi, Grimaldi; Vivaldi; Garibaldi.

-ale. See **-olly.**

-alec. See **-alic.**

-alely, bailie, daily, gaily, grayly, Haley, palely, scaly, stalely; Disraeli, Israeli, shillelagh; ukelele.

-alement. See **-ailment.**

-alent (-a-), See **-allant.**

-alent (-ā-), See **-alant.**

-aler. See **-ailer.**

-alet. See **-allot.**

-aley. See **-alely.**

-ali. See **-olly.**

-alic, Alec, Gallic, malic, phallic, salic; cephalic, italic, metallic, oxalic, vocalic; brachycephalic; dolichocephalic.

-alice. See **-allas.**

-alid (-a-), pallid, valid; invalid. See also **-alad.**

-alid (-o-). See **-olid.**

-alin. See **-allon.**

-aling. See **-ailing.**

-aliph. See **-ailiff.**

-allad. See **-alad.**

-allant. See **-alent.**

-allas, Alice, callous, chalice, Dallas, malice, palace, Pallas, phallus, talus, thallus; digitalis; aurora borealis.

-allen. See **-allon.**

-aller. See **-allor.**

-allet. See **-allot.**

-allette. See **-allot.**

-alley. See **-ally.**

-allic. See **-alic.**

-allid. See **-alid.**

-allment, appallment, enthrallment, installment; disenthrallment.

-allon, Alan, Allen, gallon, Stalin, talon; ten-gallon.

-allop (-al-), gallop, jalap, scallop, shallop; escallop.

-allop (-ol-). See **ollop.**

-allor, pallor, valor; caballer.

-allot, ballot, mallet, palate, pallet, pallette, shallot, valet.

-allow (-al-), aloe, callow, fallow, hallow, mallow, sallow, shallow, tallow; marsh-mallow.

-allow (-ol-). See **-ollow.**

-allus. See **-allas.**

-ally, alley, bally, challis, dally, galley, pally, rally, sally, Sally, tally, valley; bialy, Death Valley, finale, O'Malley; dillydally, hexicali, shillyshally.

-almest. See **-almist.**

-almist, calmest, palmist, psalmist; embalmist.

-almless, balmless, palmless, psalmless, qualmless.

-almon. See **-ammon.**

-almy. See **-ami.**

-aloe. See **-allow.**

-alon. See **-allon.**

-alor. See **-allor.**

-altar. See **-alter.**

-alter, altar, alter, falter, halter, palter, psalter, salter, vaulter, Walter; assaulter, defaulter, exalter, Gibraltar, unalter.

-alty, faulty, malty, salty, vaulty, walty.

-aly. See **-alely.**

-ama, Brahma, comma, drama, lama, llama, mama, Rama, pajama; cosmorama, Dalai Lama, diorama, docudrama, Fujiyama, georama, melodrama, neorama, panorama, Yokahama.

-ambeau. See **-ambo.**

-amber, amber, camber, clamber, tambour.

-ambit, ambit, gambit.

-amble, amble, bramble, Campbell, gamble, gambol, ramble, scamble, scramble, shamble; preamble.

-ambo, ambo, crambo, flambeau, Sambo, zambo.

-ambol. See **-amble.**

-ambour. See **-amber.**

-ameful, blameful, flameful, shameful.

-amel. See **-ammel.**

-amely, gamely, lamely, namely, tamely.

-ami, balmy, palmy, swami, Tommy; pastrami, salami, tsunami; origami.

-amin. See **-ammon.**

-amine. See **-ammon.**

-amish, Amish, famish, rammish; affamish, enfamish.

-amlet, camlet, hamlet, Hamlet, samlet.

-ammal. See **-ammel.**

-ammar. See **-ammer.**

-ammel, camel, mammal, Tamil, trammel; enamel, entrammel.

-ammer, clamor, crammer, dammer, gammer, glamour, grammar, hammer, rammer, shammer, slammer, stammer, yammer; en-

amor, jackhammer, programmer, sledge-
hammer, windjammer; katzenjammer, nin-
nyhammer, yellowhammer.

-ammish. See **-amish.**

-ammon, Ammon, famine, gamin, gammon,
mammon, salmon; examine, backgammon,
cross examine; re-examine.

-ammy, chamois, clammy, gammy, Grammy,
hammy, mammy, Sammy, shammy,
tammy; Miami.

-amois. See **-ammy.**

-amon. See **-ayman.**

-amor. See **-ammer.**

-amos. See **-amous.**

-amour. See **-ammer.**

-amous, Amos, famous, squamous, shamus;
biramous, mandamus; ignoramus; Nostra-
damus.

-ampas. See **-ampus.**

-amper, camper, cramper, damper, hamper,
pamper, scamper, stamper, tamper,
tramper.

-ample, ample, sample, trample; ensample,
example.

-ampler, ampler, sampler, trampler; exam-
pler.

-ampus, campus, grampus, pampas; hippo-
campus.

-amus. See **-amous.**

-ana (-a-), Anna, Hannah, manna; banana,
bandanna, cabana, Diana, Havana, ho-
sanna, Montana, savannah, Savannah, sultana, Urbana, Indiana, Juliana, Pollyanna,
Susquehanna; Americana, Louisiana.

-ana (-ä-), anna, Botswana, Ghana, gymkhana, iguana, nirvana, piranha, sultana, Tatiana, Tijuana, zenana; marijuana, parmigiana; fata morgana.

-anate. See **-anet.**

-ancer, answer, cancer, chancer, dancer, glancer, lancer, prancer; advancer, enhancer, entrancer, freelancer, merganser, romancer; chiromancer, geomancer, necromancer.

-ancet. See **-ansit.**

-anchion. See **-ansion.**

-anchor. See **-anker.**

-anchored. See **-ankered.**

-ancor. See **-anker.**

-ancy, chancy, Clancy, dancy, fancy, Nancy; unchancy; belomancy, chiromancy, cleromancy, consonancy, gastromancy, geomancy, gyromancy, hydromancy, lithomancy, militancy, myomancy, necromancy, onomancy, psychomancy, stichomancy, sycophancy, termagancy; aleuromancy, anthropomancy, bibliomancy, botanomancy, crystallomancy, ornithomancy, alectoromancy, alectryomancy.

-anda, panda; Amanda, Miranda, veranda; jacaranda, memoranda, propaganda.

-andal. See **-andle.**

-andant, commandant, demandant.

-andem. See **-andom.**

-ander (-an-), candor, dander, gander, grander, pander, sander, slander; backhander, bystander, commander, dittander, Leander, Lysander, meander, Menander, philander, pomander; Alexander, coriander, gerrymander, oleander, salamander.

-ander (-on-). See **-onder**.

-andhi. See **-andy**.

-andi. See **-andy**.

-andid, banded, candid, handed, landed, stranded; backhanded, high-handed, short-handed, uncandid; empty-handed, even-handed, heavy-handed, single-handed, underhanded.

-andied, bandied, brandied, candied.

-anding, banding, branding, landing, standing; demanding, disbanding, expanding, outstanding, upstanding; notwithstanding, understanding.

-andish, blandish, brandish, grandish, Standish; outlandish.

-andit, bandit, pandit.

-andle, candle, dandle, handle, sandal, scandal, vandal; manhandle, mishandle.

-andler, candler, chandler, dandler, handler; panhandler.

-andom, random, tandem; memorandum.

-andor. See **-ander**.

-andsome. See **-ansom**.

-andstand, bandstand, grandstand, handstand.

-andum. See **-andom**.

-andy, Andy, bandy, brandy, candy, dandy, Gandhi, gandy, handy, Mandy, pandy, randy, sandy, Sandy, shandy; jim-dandy, unhandy; modus operandi.

-aneful. See **-ainful**.

-anel. See **-annel**.

-anely. See **-ainly**.

-aneous, cutaneous, extraneous, spontaneous; instantaneous, miscellaneous, simultaneous; contemporaneous, extemporaneous.

-aner. See **-ainer.**

-anet, gannet, granite, Janet, planet; pomegranate.

-anger (-ang ər), anger, angor, banger, clangor, ganger, hangar, hanger, languor; haranguer, straphanger, paper hanger.

-anger (-ān jər), changer, danger, Grainger, granger, manger, ranger, stranger; arranger, bushranger, deranger, endanger, estranger, exchanger; disarranger, interchanger, money changer.

-angle, angle, bangle, brangle, dangle, jangle, mangle, spangle, strangle, tangle, twangle, wangle, wrangle; bemangle, bespangle, embrangle, entangle, quadrangle, rectangle, triangle, untangle, wide-angle; disentangle, interjangle.

-angled, newfangled, star-spangled.

  Also: **-angle** + **-ed** (as in *tangled*, etc.)

-ango, mango, tango; contango, fandango.

-angor. See **-anger.**

-anguer. See **-anger.**

-anguish, anguish, languish.

-anguor. See **-anger.**

-angy, mangy, rangy.

-anic, manic, panic, tannic; botanic, Brahmanic, Britannic, galvanic, Germanic, mechanic, organic, rhodanic, satanic, sultanic, tetanic, titanic, tyrannic, volcanic, vulcanic; aldermanic, charlatanic, diaphanic, lexiphanic, Messianic, oceanic, Ossianic, Puritanic, talismanic; ferricyanic, hydrocyanic, Indo Germanic, valerianic; interoce-anic.

-anics, annex, panics; humanics, mechanics.

-anil. See **-annel.**

-anion, banyan, canyon; companion.

-anish, banish, clannish, mannish, planish, Spanish, vanish; evanish.

-anite. See **-anet.**

-ankard. See **-ankered.**

-anker, anchor, banker, blanker, canker, chancre, clanker, danker, hanker, rancor, ranker, spanker, tanker; co-anchor.

-ankered, anchored, cankered, hankered, tankard.

-ankle, ankle, rankle.

-ankly, blankly, dankly, frankly, lankly, rankly.

-anna. See **-ana.**

-annah. See **-ana.**

-annal. See **-annel.**

-annel, anil, annal, cannel, channel, flannel, panel, scrannel; empanel.

-anner, banner, canner, manner, manor, planner, scanner, spanner, tanner.

-annet. See **-anet.**

-annex. See **-anics.**

-annic. See **-anic.**

-annie. See **-anny.**

-annish. See **-anish.**

-annual. See **-anual.**

-anny, Annie, canny, clanny, cranny, Danny, fanny, Fanny, granny, Mannie, nanny; un-canny; frangipani, hootenanny.

-anor. See **-anner.**

-anser. See **-ancer.**

-ansett. See **-ansit.**

-ansion, mansion, scansion, stanchion; expansion.

-ansit, lancet, transit; Narragansett.

-ansom, handsome, hansom, ransom, transom; unhandsome.

-answer. See **-ancer.**

-ansy, pansy, tansy; chimpanzee.

-anta, Santa; Atlanta, infanta, Vedanta; Atalanta.

-antam, bantam, phantom.

-ante. See **-anty.**

-anteau. See **-anto.**

-antel. See **-antle.**

-anter, banter, canter, cantor, chanter, grantor, panter, planter, ranter; decanter, descanter, enchanter, implanter, instanter, Levanter, recanter, transplanter, trochanter.

-anther, anther, panther.

-anti. See **-anty.**

-antic, antic, frantic, mantic; Atlantic, bacchantic, gigantic, pedantic, romantic; chiromantic, consonantic, corybantic, geomantic, hierophantic, hydromantic, necromantic, pyromantic, sycophantic, transatlantic.

-antine, Byzantine, Levantine; adamantine, elephantine.

-antle, cantle, mantel, mantle, scantle; immantle.

-antler, antler, mantler, pantler; dismantler.

-antling, bantling, mantling, scantling; dismantling.

-anto, canto, panto; coranto, portmanteau; Esperanto, quo warranto.

-antom. See **-antam.**

-antor. See **-anter.**

-antry, chantry, gantry, pantry.

-anty, ante, anti, auntie, chanty, Dante, scanty, shanty; Ashanti, Bacchante, andante, chianti, infante; dilettante, vigilante.

-anual, annual, manual; Emmanuel.

-anuel. See **-anual.**

-any (-ā-). See **-ainy.**

-any (-e-). See **-enny.**

-anyan. See **-anion.**

-anyon. See **-anion.**

-anza, stanza; bonanza; Sancho Panza; extravaganza.

-anzee. See **-ansy.**

-aoler. See **-ailer.**

-apal. See **-aple.**

-ape. See **-appy.**

-apel. See **-apple.**

-apen, capon; misshapen, unshapen.

-aper, caper, draper, paper, sapor, taper, tapir, vapor; flypaper, landscaper, newspaper, sandpaper, skyscraper.

-aphic, graphic, traffic; seraphic; autographic, biographic, calligraphic, cartographic, chirographic, cosmographic, crytographic, diagraphic, epigraphic, epitaphic, ethnographic, geographic, hierographic, holographic, hydrographic, lithographic, monographic, orthographic, pantographic, paragraphic, petrographic, phonographic, photographic, polygraphic, pornographic, scenographic, seismographic, stenographic, stratigraphic, stylographic, telegraphic, topographic, typographic, xylographic; bibliographic, choreographic, heliographic, heterographic, ideographic, lexicographic, physiographic; autobiographic, cinematographic.

-apid, rapid, sapid, vapid.

-apir. See **-aper.**

-apist, papist, rapist; escapist, landscapist.

-aple, maple, papal, staple.

-apless, capless, hapless, napless, sapless, strapless.

-apling. See **-appling.**

-apnel, grapnel, shrapnel.

-apon. See **-apen.**

-apor. See **-aper.**

-apper, capper, clapper, dapper, flapper, mapper, napper, sapper, tapper, trapper, wrapper; entrapper, fly-sapper, kidnapper, wiretapper; handicapper, understrapper, whippersnapper.

-appet, lappet, tappet.

-appie. See **-appy.**

-apple, apple, chapel, dapple, grapple, scapple, scrapple, thrapple; love apple, pineapple.

-appling, dappling, grappling, sapling.

-appy, chappie, flappy, happy, knappy, nappy, sappy, scrappy, snappy; serape, slap-happy, unhappy.

-apter, apter, captor, chapter; adapter, recaptor.

-aptest. See **-aptist.**

-aption, caption; adaption, contraption, recaption.

-aptist, aptest, baptist, raptest; adaptest, inaptest; anabaptist.

-aptor. See **-apter.**

-apture, capture, rapture; enrapture, recapture.

-ara, Clara, Sarah; mascara, tiara.

-arab, arab, Arab, carob, scarab.

-arage. See **-arriage.**

-araoh. See **-arrow.**

-arass. See **-arras.**

-arat. See **-aret.**

-arbel. See **-arble.**

-arber. See **-arbor.**

-arbered. See **-arboard.**

-arble (-är-), barbel, garbel, garble, marble; enmarble.

-arble (-ôr-), corbel, warble.

-arboard, barbered, harbored, larboard, starboard.

-arbor, arbor, barber, harbor.

-arbored. See **-arboard.**

-arcel, parcel, sarcel, tarsal; metatarsal.

-archal. See **-arkle.**

-archer, archer, marcher, parcher, starcher; departure.

-archy, barky, darky, larky, marquee, sparky; malarkey; heterarchy, hierarchy, matriarchy, oligarchy, patriarchy.

-arden (-är-), Arden, garden, harden, pardon; beer-garden, bombardon, caseharden, enharden.

-arden (-ôr-). See **-ordon.**

-arder (-är-), ardor, carder, harder, larder; bombarder, Cunarder.

-arder (-ôr-). See **-order.**

-ardon. See **-arden.**

-ardor. See **-arder.**

-ardy, hardy, lardy, tardy; foolhardy, Lombardy, Picardy.

-arel. See **-arrel.**

-arely, barely, fairly, rarely, squarely, yarely; unfairly; debonairly.

-arent, arrant, parent; apparent, transparent.

-aret, carat, caret, carrot, claret, garret, karat, parrot.

-arfish, garfish, starfish.

-argent, argent, sergeant.

-arger, charger, larger; enlarger.

-argo, Argo, argot, cargo, largo, Margot; botargo, embargo, Wells Fargo; supercargo.

-argot. See **-argo.**

-ari (-âr-). See **-ary.**

-ari (-är-). See **-arry.**

-arian. See **-arion.**

-aric, baric, carrick, Garrick; agaric, barbaric, Pindaric; Balearic, cinnabaric, hyperbaric, isobaric. See also **-arrack.**

-arid. See **-arried.**

-aried. See **-arried.**

-arier. See **-arrier.**

-aring, airing, bearing, daring, fairing, glaring, raring, wearing; seafaring, talebearing, uncaring, unsparing, wayfaring; overbearing.

-arion, Arian, Aryan, carrion, clarion, Marian, Marion.

-arious, Darius, various; Aquarius, bifarious, contrarious, gregarious, hilarious, nefari-

ous, ovarious, precarious, vicarious; multi-
farious, Sagittarius, temerarious.

-aris, Paris, Harris; embarrass, Polaris. See
also **-arras.**

-arish, barish, bearish, garish, parish, rarish,
sparish, squarish; debonairish.

-arius. See **-arious.**

-arken, darken, hearken.

-arkish, darkish, larkish, sparkish.

-arkle, darkle, sparkle; monarchal; patriar-
chal.

-arkling, darkling, sparkling.

-arkly, darkly, sparkly, starkly.

-arky. See **-archy.**

-arler, gnarler, marler, parlor, snarler.

-arlet, carlet, harlot, scarlet, starlet, varlet.

-arley. See **-arly.**

-arlic, garlic, Harlech, pilgarlic.

-arlie. See **-arly.**

-arling, darling, marling, snarling, sparling,
starling.

-arlor. See **-arler.**

-arlot. See **-arlet.**

-arly, barley, Charlie, gnarly, parley, snarly;
particularly.

-armer, armor, charmer, farmer; snake
charmer.

-arming, arming, charming, farming; alarm-
ing, disarming.

-armless, armless, charmless, harmless.

-armor. See **-armer.**

-army, army, barmy, swarmy.

-arnel, carnal, charnel, darnel.

-arner, garner, harner; Silas Marner.

-arning. See **-orning.**

-arnish, garnish, tarnish, varnish.

-aro (-á-), pharoah, taro; bolero, dinero, primero, sombrero, torero; caballero; banderillero, embarcadero. See also **-arrow.**

-arol. See **-arrel.**

-aron, Aaron, baron, barren, Charon, marron, Sharon; rose of Sharon.

-arper, harper, sharper.

-arquee. See **-archy.**

-arrack, arrack, barrack, carrack. See also **-aric.**

-arrant. See **-arent.**

-arras, arras, harass; embarrass. See also **-aris.**

-arrel (-ar-), barrel, carol, Carol, carrel, Carroll; apparel.

-arrel (-ôr-). See **-oral.**

-arret. See **-aret.**

-arriage, carriage, marriage; disparage, miscarriage, mismarriage; intermarriage.

-arrick. See **-aric.**

-arrie. See **-ary.**

-arried, arid, carried, harried, married, parried, tarried, varied; miscarried, remarried, unmarried, unvaried; intermarried.

-arrier, barrier, carrier, charier, farrier, harrier, marrier, parrier, tarrier.

-arrion. See **-arion.**

-arris. See **-aris.**

-arron. See **-aron.**

-arrot. See **-aret.**

-arrow, arrow, barrow, faro, farrow, harrow,

Harrow, marrow, narrow, Pharaoh, sparrow, taro, yarrow. See also **-aro.**

-arry (-är-), charry, sari, scarry, sparry, starry; aracari, carbonari, hari-kari, Mata Hari. See also **-orry.**

-arry (-âr-). See **-ary.**

-arsal. See **-arcel.**

-arshal. See **-artial.**

-arsley, parsley, sparsley.

-arson, arson, Carson, parson.

-artan. See **-arten.**

-arte. See **-arty.**

-arten, barton, carton, hearten, marten, martin, Martin, smarten, Spartan, tartan; dishearten; kindergarten.

-arter, barter, carter, charter, darter, garter, martyr, starter, tartar; nonstarter, self-starter, upstarter.

-artful, artful, cartful, heartful.

-artial, marshal, Marshall, martial, partial; court martial, immartial, impartial.

-artin. See **-arten.**

-artist, artist, Chartist, smartest.

-artly, partly, smartly, tartly.

-arton. See **-arten.**

-artridge, cartridge, partridge.

-arture. See **-archer.**

-arty, arty, hearty, party, smarty; Astarte, ex parte, Havarti; commedia del l'arte.

-artyr. See **-arter.**

-arval. See **-arvel.**

-arvel, carvel, larval, marvel.

-arving, carving, starving.

-ary, aerie, airy, Carrie, carry, chary, dairy,

eyrie, fairy, Gary, hairy, harry, Larry,
marry, Mary, merry, nary, parry, prairie,
scary, tarry, vary, wary; canary, contrary,
miscarry, unchary, unwary, vagary; actu-
ary, adversary, ancillary, antiquary, arbi-
trary, capillary, cassowary, cautionary,
centenary, commentary, commissary, cor-
ollary, culinary, customary, dictionary, die-
tary, dignitary, dromedary, estuary, Febru-
ary, formulary, functionary, hari-kari,
honorary, intermarry, Janissary, January,
legendary, legionary, literary, luminary,
mercenary, military, momentary, mone-
tary, mortuary, necessary, ordinary, pas-
sionary, planetary, prebendary, pulmonary,
reliquary, salivary, salutary, sanctuary,
sanguinary, sanitary, scapulary, secondary,
secretary, sedentary, seminary, solitary,
stationary, statuary, sublunary, sumptuary,
temporary, tertiary, Tipperary, titulary,
tributary, tumulary, tutelary, visionary,
voluntary, vulnerary; ablutionary, accusto-
mary, additionary, adminculary, apothe-
cary, confectionary, constabulary, contem-
porary, contributary, depositary, epistolary,
fiduciary, hereditary, imaginary, incendi-
ary, involuntary, obituary, pecuniary, proprietary, residuary, ubiquitary, vocabulary,
voluptuary; accidentiary, beneficiary, evo-
lutionary, extraordinary, intermediary. See
also **-erry.**

-aryan. See **-arion.**

-asal, basal, basil, hazel, nasal, phrasal; ap-
praisal, witch hazel.

-ascal, paschal, rascal.

-ascar. See **-asker.**

-ascence, nascence; complacence, obeisance, renascence.

-ascent. See **-acent.**

-asement, basement, casement, placement; abasement, debasement, defacement, displacement, effacement, embracement, enlacement, erasement, misplacement, retracement, subbasement; interlacement.

-aser. See **-azer.**

-asey. See **-acy.**

-asher, Asher, basher, Dasher, flasher, masher, rasher, slasher, smasher, splasher, thrasher; gatecrasher; haberdasher.

-ashion. See **-assion.**

-ashy (-a-), ashy, flashy, mashie, mashy, plashy, slashy, splashy, trashy.

-ashy (-o-). See **-oshy.**

-asian. See **-asion.**

-asion, Asian, suasion; abrasion, Caucasian, dissuasion, equation, Eurasian, evasion, invasion, occasion, persuasion, pervasion; Rabelaisian.

-asis (-ā-), basis, crasis, glacis, phasis, stasis; oasis.

-asive, suasive; assuasive, dissuasive, evasive, invasive, persuasive, pervasive.

-asker, asker, basker, lascar, masker; Madagascar.

-asket, basket, casket, flasket, gasket.

-ason. See **-asten.**

-aspar. See **-asper.**

-asper, asper, Caspar, gasper, jasper, Jasper. Also: **-asp** + **-er** (as in *clasper,* etc.)

-assal. See **-astle.**

-assel. See **-astle.**

-asses, molasses.

> Also: **-ass** + **-es** (as in *classes*, etc.)

-asset, asset, basset, brasset, facet, tacit.

-assic, classic; boracic, Jurassic, potassic, sebacic, thoracic, Triassic.

-assie. See **-assy.**

-assion, ashen, fashion, passion, ration; Circassian, compassion, dispassion, impassion.

-assive, massive, passive; impassive.

-assle. See **-astle.**

-assock, cassock, hassock.

-assy, brassie, brassy, chassis, classy, gassy, glassy, grassy, lassie, massy, sassy; morassy; Malagasy, Tallahassee; Haile Selassie.

-astard, bastard, castored, dastard, mastered, plastered.

-asten (-ā-), basin, caisson, chasten, hasten, mason.

-asten (-a-), fasten; assassin, unfasten.

-aster (-ā-), baster, chaster, haster, paster, taster, waster.

-aster (-a-), aster, Astor, blaster, caster, castor, faster, master, pastor, piaster, plaster, vaster; bandmaster, cadaster, disaster, headmaster, ringmaster, schoolmaster, spymaster, taskmaster; alabaster, burgomaster, concertmaster, criticaster, medicaster, oleaster, overmaster, poetaster, quartermaster, Zoroaster.

-astered. See **-astard.**

-astic, drastic, mastic, plastic, spastic; bombastic, dichastic, dynastic, elastic, emplastic, fantastic, gymnastic, monastic, sarcastic, scholastic; anaclastic, antiphrastic, chiliastic, inelastic, metaphrastic, onomastic, orgiastic, paraphrastic, periphrastic, pleonastic, protoplastic, scholiastic; ecclesiastic, enthusiastic, iconoclastic.

-asting, everlasting.

    Also: **-ast + -ing** (as in *fasting*, etc.)

-astle, castle, facile, hassle, Kassel passel, tassel, vassal, wassail, wrastle; forecastle, Newcastle.

-astly, ghastly, lastly, vastly.

-astor. See **-aster.**

-astored. See **-astard.**

-asty (-as-), blasty, nasty, vasty.

-asty (-ās-), hasty, pasty, tasty.

-asy. See **-assy.**

-ata (-ätə), beta, data, eta, strata, theta, zeta; albata, dentata, errata, pro rata; postulata, ultimata, vertebrata; invertebrata.

-ata (-ätə), data, strata; cantata, errata, frittata, pinata, regatta, sonata, toccata; caponata, serenata, terra cotta; inamorata; persona non grata.

-atal, datal, fatal, natal, statal; postnatal; antenatal, neonatal, perinatal.

-atan, Satan, straighten, straiten.

-atant. See **-atent.**

-atcher, catcher, matcher, patcher, scratcher, snatcher, stature, thatcher; dispatcher, detacher, flycatcher.

-atchet, hatchet, latchet, ratchet.

-atchman, Scotchman, watchman.

-atchment, catchment, hatchment, ratchment; attachment, detachment, dispatchment.

-ateau, château, plateau. See also **-ato** (-ä-).

-ateful, fateful, grateful, hateful, plateful.

-atent, blatant, latent, natant, patent.

-ater (-ô-), daughter, slaughter, tauter, water; backwater, dishwater, firewater, granddaughter, manslaughter, rainwater, rosewater, stepdaughter.

-ater (-ā-). See **-ator.**

-ather (-a*th*-), blather, Cather, gather, lather, Mather, rather, slather; foregather.

-ather (-o*th*-). See **-other.**

-athos, Athos, bathos, pathos.

-ati (-ä-), basmati, gelati, karate, Scarlatti; digerati, glitterati, literati.

-atial. See **-acial.**

-atian. See **-ation.**

-atic, attic, static; aquatic, astatic, asthmatic, chromatic, climatic, Dalmatic, dogmatic, dramatic, ecbatic, ecstatic, emphatic, erratic, fanatic, hepatic, lymphatic, phlegmatic, piratic, pneumatic, pragmatic, prismatic, quadratic, rheumatic, Socratic, stigmatic, thematic, traumatic; achromatic, acrobatic, Adriatic, aerostatic, aplanatic, aromatic, Asiatic, autocratic, automatic, bureaucratic, democratic, dichromatic, diplomatic, eleatic, emblematic, enigmatic, Hanseatic, hieratic, hydrostatic, mathematic, morganatic, numismatic, operatic, pancreatic, plutocratic, problematic, symptomatic, systematic; anagrammatic, aristocratic, axiomatic, epigrammatic, idiocratic, idiomatic, melodramatic, physiocratic, psychosomatic, undiplomatic; idiosyncratic.

-atim, verbatim, literatim, seriatim. See also **-atum.**

-atin, matin, Latin, patin, platen, satin; Manhattan, Powhattan. See also **-atten.**

-ation, Haitian, nation, ration, station; ablation, aeration, Alsatian, carnation, castration, causation, cessation, citation, collation, creation, cremation, Dalmatian, damnation, deflation, dictation, dilation, donation, duration, elation, equation, filtration, fixation, flirtation, flotation, formation, foundation, frustration, gestation, gradation, gyration, hortation, inflation, lactation, laudation, lavation, legation, libation, location, migration, mutation, narration, negation, notation, nugation, oblation, oration, ovation, plantation, predation, privation, probation, prostration, pulsation, quotation, relation, rogation, rotation, sensation, serration, stagnation, taxation, temptation, translation, vacation, venation, vexation, vibration, vocation; abdication, aberration, abjuration, abnegation, abrogation, acceptation, acclamation, accusation, actuation, adaptation, adjuration, admiration, adoration, adulation, adumbration, aerostation, affectation, affirmation, aggravation, aggregation, agitation, allegation, allocation, alteration, altercation, alternation, angulation, amputation, animation, annexation, annotation, appellation, application, approbation, arbitration, arrogation, aspiration, assignation, association, attestation, augmentation, aviation, avocation, bifurcation, calcination, calculation, cancellation, captivation, castigation, celebration, circulation, cogitation, collocation, coloration, combination, commendation, commutation, compensation, compilation, complication, computation, concentration, condemnation, condensation, confirmation, confiscation, conflagration, conformation, confrontation, confutation, congregation, conjugation, conjuration, connotation, consecration, conservation, consolation, constellation, consternation, consultation, consummation, contemplation, conversation, convocation, copulation, coronation, corporation, correlation, corrugation, coruscation, culmination, cultivation, cumulation, debarkation, decimation, declamation, declaration, declination, decoration, dedication, defalcation, defamation, defloration, deformation, degradation, delectation, delegation, demonstration, denotation, denudation, depilation, deportation, depravation, deprecation, depredation, deprivation, deputation, derivation, derogation, desecration, desiccation, designation, desolation, desperation, destination, detestation, detonation, devastation, deviation, dislocation, dispensation, disputation, dissertation, dissipation, distillation; divination, domination, duplication, education, elevation, elongation, emanation, emendation, emigration, emulation, enervation, equitation, eructation, estimation, estivation, evocation, exaltation, excavation, excitation, exclamation, execration, exhalation, exhortation, expectation, expiation, expiration, explanation, explication, exploitation, exploration, exportation, expurgation, extirpation, exultation, fabrication, fascination, federation, fenestration, fermentation, flagellation, fluctuation, fomentation, fornication, fulmination, fumigation, generation, germination, graduation, granulation, gravitation, habitation, hesitation, hibernation, ideation, illustration, imitation, implantation, implication, importation, imprecation, impregnation, incantation, incitation, inclination, incubation, inculcation, indentation, indication, indignation, infestation, infiltration, inflammation, information, inhalation, innovation, inspiration, installation, instigation, instillation, intimation, intonation, inundation, invitation, invocation, irrigation, irritation, isolation, jubilation, laceration, lamentation, lamination, legislation, levitation, liberation, limitation, litigation, lubrication, lucubration, maceration, machination, malformation, mastication, maturation, mediation, medication, meditation, menstruation, mensuration, ministration, mitigation, moderation, modulation, molestation, mutilation, navigation, numeration, obfuscation, objurgation, obligation, obscuration, observation, obviation, occupation, operation, ordination, orchestration, oscillation, palpitation, penetration, percolation, perforation, permeation, permutation, peroration, perpetration, perspiration, perturbation, population, postulation, predication, preparation, presentation, preservation, proclamation, procreation, procuration, profanation, profligation, prolongation, protestation, provocation, publication, punctuation, radiation, recitation, reclamation, recreation, reformation, refutation, registration, regulation, relaxation, remonstration, renovation, reparation, reputation, reservation, resignation, respiration, restoration, retardation, revelation, revocation, ruination, rumination, rustication, salutation, scintillation, segmentation, segregation, separation, sequestration, simulation, situation, speculation, spoliation, stimulation, sublimation, subornation, suffocation, supplication, suppuration, suspiration, syncopation, termination, titillation, toleration, transformation, transplantation, transportation, trepidation, tribulation, triplication, usurpation, vaccination, vacillation, valuation, variation, vegetation, veneration, ventilation, vindication, violation, visitation, vitiation; abbreviation, abomination, acceleration, accentuation, accommodation, accreditation, accumulation, adjudication, administration, adulteration, affiliation, agglutination, alienation, alleviation, alliteration, amalgamation, amplification, annihilation, annunciation, anticipation, appreciation, appropriation, approximation, argumentation, articulation, asphyxiation, assassination, assimilation, attenuation, authorization, brutalization, calcification, calumniation, canonization, capitulation, carbonization, catechization, clarification, coagulation, codification, cohabitation, columniation, commemoration, commensuration, commiseration, communication, concatenation, conciliation, confederation, configuration, conglomeration, congratula-

tion, consideration, consolidation, contami-
nation, continuation, cooperation, coordi-
nation, corroboration, crystallization,
debilitation, degeneration, deification, de-
liberation, delimitation, delineation, de-
nomination, denunciation, depopulation,
depreciation, despoliation, determination,
dignification, dilapidation, disapprobation,
discoloration, discrimination, disfiguration,
disinclination, disintegration, dissemina-
tion, disseveration, dissimulation, dissocia-
tion, documentation, domestication, edifi-
cation, effectuation, ejaculation,
elaboration, elimination, elucidation, ema-
ciation, emancipation, emasculation, em-
barkation, enumeration, enunciation,
equalization, equilibration, equivocation,
eradication, evacuation, evaporation, evis-
ceration, exacerbation, exaggeration, exam-
ination, exasperation, excoriation, exhilara-
tion, exoneration, expatiation,
expectoration, expostulation, expropriation,
extenuation, extermination, facilitation, fal-
sification, felicitation, fertilization, fortifica-
tion, fossilization, galvanization, gesticula-
tion, glorification, gratification,
habilitation, habituation, hallucination,
harmonization, Hellenization, humiliation,
hypothecation, idealization, illumination,
imagination, immoderation, inauguration,
incarceration, incineration, incorporation,
incrimination, inebriation, infatuation, ini-
tiation, inoculation, insemination, insinua-
tion, interpolation, interpretation, interro-
gation, intoxication, investigation,
irradiation, justification, legalization, legiti-

mation, manifestation, manipulation, matriculation, melioration, misinformation, modernization, modification, mollification, moralization, mortification, multiplication, mystification, nasalization, negotiation, notification, obliteration, origination, organization, ossification, pacification, participation, perambulation, peregrination, perpetuation, precipitation, predestination, predomination, premeditation, preoccupation, prevarication, procrastination, prognostication, pronunciation, propitiation, protuberation, purification, qualification, ramification, ratification, realization, reciprocation, recommendation, recrimination, rectification, recuperation, refrigeration, regeneration, regurgitation, reiteration, rejuvenation, remuneration, renunciation, representation, repudiation, resuscitation, retaliation, reverberation, sanctification, scarification, signification, solemnization, sophistication, specialization, specification, subordination, symbolization, variegation, versification, vituperation, vivification, vociferation; amelioration, beatification, circumnavigation, contraindication, crossexamination, demonetization, deterioration, differentiation, discontinuation, disqualification, diversification, electrification, excommunication, exemplification, experimentation, extemporization, identification, inconsideration, indemnification, individuation, misrepresentation, naturalization, personification, predetermination, prestidigitation, ratiocination, recapitulation, reconciliation, spiritualization, super-

annuation, supererogation, tintinnabulation, transubstantiation.

-atius. See **-acious.**

-ative, dative, native, stative; creative, dila-
tive; aggregative, cogitative, cumulative,
designative, emulative, estimative, generative, hesitative, imitative, innovative, legislative, meditative, operative, predicative,
procreative, quantitative, radiative, speculative, terminative, vegetative, violative;
appreciative, associative, communicative,
continuative, corroborative, degenerative,
deliberative, determinative, discriminative,
exonerative, illuminative, interpretative, investigative, obliterative, premeditative, recuperative, regenerative, vituperative.

-atling. See **-attling.**

-atly, flatly, patly, rattly.

-ato (-ā-), Cato, Plato; potato, tomato.

-ato (-ä-), legato, mulatto, tomato, staccato;
obbligato, pizzicato; inamorato. See also
-otto.

-ator (-ā-), cater, crater, freighter, gaiter, ga-
tor, greater, later, mater, pater, satyr, tater,
traitor, waiter; creator, cunctator, curator,
Decatur, dictator, dumbwaiter, equator,
first-rater, spectator, testator, third-rater;
alligator, alma mater, carburetor, commen-
tator, conservator, elevator, fascinator,
galdiator, second-rater; perambulator.

　　Also: **-ate** + **-er** or **-or** (as in *hater, cul-
　　tivator, impersonator, procrastinator,*
　　etc.)

-atron, matron, natron, patron, waitron.

-atten, baton, batten, fatten, flatten, paten, platen, ratten. See also **-atin.**

-atter (-a-), attar, batter, blatter, chatter, clatter, fatter, flatter, hatter, latter, matter, patter, ratter, satyr, scatter, shatter, smatter, spatter, splatter, tatter; bescatter, bespatter, Mad Hatter.

-atter (-o-). See **-otter.**

-attern, pattern, Saturn, slattern.

-attle (-a-), battle, cattle, chattel, prattle, rattle, tattle; embattle, Seattle; tittle-tattle.

-attle (-o-). See **-ottle.**

-attler, battler, rattler, Statler, tattler.

-attling, battling, fatling, gatling, rattling, spratling, tattling.

-atto. See **-ato.**

-atty, batty, chatty, fatty, gnatty, Hattie, matty, natty, patty, ratty, scatty; Cincinnati.

-atum, datum, stratum; erratum, substratum, verbatim; seriatim, ultimatum; desideratum. See also **-atim.**

-ature (-ā-), nature; plicature; legislature, nomenclature.

-ature (-a-). See **-atcher.**

-aturn. See **-attern.**

-atus (-ā-), status, stratus; afflatus, hiatus, senatus; apparatus, literatus.

-atus (-a-), gratis, lattice, status; clematis; apparatus.

-aty, eighty, Haiti, Katie, matey, platy, praty, slaty, weighty.

-atyr. See **-atter.**

-audal. See **-awdle.**

-audit, audit, plaudit.

-audy. See **-awdy.**
-auger (-ā-). See **-ager.**
-augher (-af-). See **-affer.**
-aughter (-af-). See **-after.**
-aughter (-ô-). See **-ater.**
-aughty, haughty, naughty.
-aulic, aulic; hydraulic; interaulic.
-aulter. See **-alter.**
-aulty. See **-alty.**
-aunder, launder, maunder.
-aunter, flaunter, gaunter, haunter, jaunter, saunter, taunter, vaunter.
-auntie. See **-anty.**
-auphin. See **-often.**
-aural. See **-oral.**
-aurel. See **-oral.**
-aurus. See **-orous.**
-auseous. See **-autious.**
-austral, austral, claustral.
-aution, caution; incaution, precaution.
-autious, cautious, nauseous; precautious.
-ava, brava, fava, guava, Java, lava; cassava; balaclava.
-avage, ravage, savage, scavage.
-avel, cavil, gavel, gravel, ravel, travail, travel; unravel.
-avelin, javelin, ravelin.
-aveling, knaveling, shaveling.
-avely, bravely, gravely, knavely, slavely, suavely.
-avement, lavement, pavement; depravement, engravement, enslavement.
-aven, craven, graven, haven, mavin, raven, shaven; engraven, New Haven; riboflavin.

-aver (-a-), cadaver, palaver.

-aver (-ā-), braver, craver, favor, flavor, graver, haver, quaver, raver, savor, shaver, slaver, waiver, waver; disfavor, engraver, enslaver, papaver, lifesaver, timesaver; demiquaver, hemiquaver, semiquaver; hemidemisemiquaver.

-avern, cavern, tavern.

-avid, avid, gravid, pavid; impavid.

-avior, pavior, savior, Xavier; behavior; misbehavior.

-avis, Davis, mavis; rara avis.

-avish (-ā-), bravish, knavish, slavish.

-avish (-a-), lavish, ravish; enravish, MacTavish.

-avo, bravo; centavo, octavo.

-avor. See **-aver.**

-avy, cavy, Davy, gravy, navy, slavey, wavy; peccavi.

-awdle, caudal, dawdle.

-awdry, Audrey, bawdry, tawdry.

-awdy, bawdy, dawdy, gaudy.

-awful, awful, lawful; unlawful.

-awning, awning, dawning, fawning, spawning, yawning.

-awny, brawny, fawny, lawny, Pawnee, scrawny, Shawnee, tawny, yawny; mulligatawny.

-awyer, foyer, lawyer, sawyer; topsawyer.

-axen, flaxen, Jackson, klaxon, Saxon, waxen; Anglo-Saxon.

-axi. See **-axy.**

-axon. See **-axen.**

-axy, flaxy, taxi, waxy; galaxy; ataraxy, Cotopaxi.

-aybe. See **-aby.**

-ayday, heyday, Mayday, payday, playday.

-ayer, layer, mayor, prayer; purveyor, soothsayer, surveyor.
  Also: **-ay** + **-er** (as in *player,* etc.)

-ayey, clayey, wheyey.

-aylay, Malay, melee, waylay; ukulele.

-ayling. See **-ailing.**

-ayman, Bremen, cayman, Damon, drayman, Haman, layman, Lehman, stamen; highwayman.

-ayment, claimant, payment, raiment; defrayment, displayment, repayment.

-ayo, kayo, Mayo.

-aza, Gaza, plaza; piazza; tabula rasa.

-azard, hazard, mazzard; haphazard.

-azel. See **-asal.**

-azen. See **-azon.**

-azer, blazer, gazer, maser, phaser, praiser, razor; appraiser fundraiser, hellraiser, stargazer, trailblazer; paraphraser.

-azier, brazier, glazier, grazier.

-azon, blazon, brazen, glazen, raisin; emblazon; diapason.

-azy, crazy, daisy, hazy, lazy, Maisie, mazy; stir-crazy.

-azzle, basil, dazzle, frazzle, razzle; bedazzle; razzle-dazzle.

-ea, Leah, Mia, zea; Althea, chorea, Crimea, idea, Judea, Korea, Maria, Medea, obeah, Sofia, spirea, tortilla; Caesarea, Cytherea, dahabeah, diarrhea, gonorrhea, Latakia, panacea, pizzeria, ratafia, sinfonia, Tanza-

nia, trattoria; Andalucia, Arimathea, bou-
gainvillea, Cassiopeia, cavalleria, pharma-
copoeia; onomatopoeia.

-eaboard, keyboard, seaboard.

-eacher, beacher, bleacher, breacher, bree-
cher, creature, feature, leacher, peacher,
preacher, reacher, screecher, teacher; be-
seecher, impeacher.

-eachment, preachment; impeachment.

-eachy, beachy, lichee, litchi, Nietzsche,
peachy, preachy, screechy; Campeche.

-eacon, beacon, deacon, weaken; archdea-
con, Mohican, subdeacon.

-eaden, deaden, leaden, redden, threaden;
Armageddon.

-eading. See **-edding.**

-eadle (-ē-). See **-eedle.**

-eadle (-e-). See **-eddle.**

-eadlock, deadlock, headlock, wedlock.

-eadly, deadly, medley, redly.

-eady. See **-eedy.**

-eafer. See **-ephyr.**

-eager, eager, leaguer, meager; beleaguer,
intriguer; overeager.

-eah. See **-ea.**

-eaken. See **-eacon.**

-eaker. See **-aker.**

-eakly, bleakly, meekly, sleekly, treacly,
weakly, weekly; biweekly, obliquely,
uniquely; semiweekly.

-ealment, concealment, congealment, repeal-
ment, revealment.

-ealot. See **-ellate.**

-ealous, Hellas, jealous, trellis, zealous; apellous, entellus, Marcellus, procellous, vitellus.

-ealy. See **-eely.**

-eamer, dreamer, emir, femur, lemur, reamer, schemer, steamer, streamer; blasphemer, redeemer.

-eamish, beamish, squeamish.

-eamster, deemster, seamster, teamster.

-ean, eon, Ian, Leon, lien, paean; Achaean, Aegean, Andean, astrean, Augean, Chaldean, Crimean, Judean, Korean, Lethean, nymphean, pampean, plebian, protean; amoebean, amphigean, apogean, Caribbean, empyrean, European, Galilean, Herculean, Jacobean, Maccabean, Manichaean, Mycenaean, Odyssean, perigean, Sisyphean, Tennessean; adamantean, antipodean, epicurean, Pythagorean, terpsichorean.

-eaner, cleaner, gleaner, greener, meaner, wiener; demeanor, machiner; misdemeanor.

-eaning, gleaning, meaning.
    Also: **-ean** + **-ing** (as in *cleaning*, etc.)
    Also: **-een** + **-ing** (as in *preening*, etc.)
    Also: **-ene** + **-ing** (as in *intervening*, etc.)
    Also: **-ine** + **-ing** (as in *machining*, etc.)

-eanly, cleanly, keenly, leanly, meanly, queenly; obscenely, routinely, serenely.

-eanor. See **-eaner.**

-eany. See **-eeny.**

-eapen. See **-eepen.**

-eaper. See **-eeper.**

-earage. See **-eerage.**

-earance, clearance; adherence, appearance, arrearance, coherence, inherence; disappearance, incoherence, interference, perseverance.

-earful, cheerful, earful, fearful, sneerful.

-earing (-ir-), Bering, earring; God-fearing; hard-of-hearing.
    Also: **-ear + -ing** (as in *clearing,* etc.)
    Also: **-eer + -ing** (as in *engineering,* etc.)
    Also: **-ere + -ing** (as in *adhering,* etc.)

-earing (-âr-). See **-aring.**

-earish. See **-arish.**

-early (-ir-). See **-erely.**

-early (-ûr-). See **-urly.**

-earner, burner, earner, learner, turner; sojourner.

-earnest, earnest, Ernest, sternest; internist.

-earning, burning, churning, earning, learning, spurning, turning, yearning; concerning, discerning, returning.

-earsal. See **-ersal.**

-earten. See **-arten.**

-eartener. See **-artner.**

-eartlet. See **-artlet.**

-earty. See **-arty.**

-eary, aerie, beery, bleary, cheery, dearie, dreary, eerie, Erie, jeery, leery, peri, query, smeary, sneery, sphery, veery, weary; aweary, Lake Erie, Valkyrie, world-weary; miserere.

-easant (-ez-), peasant, pheasant, pleasant, present; unpleasant; omnipresent.

-easants. See **-esence.**

-easel, Diesel, easel, measle, teasel, weasel.

-easer (-ēz-), Caesar, easer, freezer, friezer, geezer, pleaser, sneezer, squeezer, teaser, tweezer, wheezer; crowd-pleaser, Ebenezer.

-easer (-ēs-), greaser, leaser, piecer; increaser, two-piecer.

-easing (-ēz-), breezing, easing, freezing, pleasing, sneezing, squeezing, teasing; appeasing, displeasing, unpleasing.

-easing (-ēs-), fleecing; increasing, subleasing, surceasing.

-eason, reason, season, treason; unreason.

-easoned, reasoned, seasoned, treasoned, weasand; unseasoned.

-easter, Easter, feaster; northeaster, southeaster.

-easting, bee-sting, easting, feasting.

-eastly, beastly, priestly, Priestly.

-easure (-e-), leisure, measure, pleasure, treasure; admeasure, displeasure, entreasure, outmeasure, countermeasure.

-easy (-ē si), creasy, fleecy, greasy, specie.

-easy (-ē zi), breezy, cheesy, easy, freezy, greasy, queasy, sleazy, sneezy, wheezy; parcheesi, speakeasy, uneasy, Zambezi.

-eaten, beaten, Cretan, cretin, eaten, Eton, heaten, sweeten, wheaten; browbeaten, moth-eaten, storm-beaten, unbeaten, worm-eaten; overeaten, weather-beaten.

-eater (-ē-), beater, cheater, eater, greeter, heater, liter, litre, meter, metre, neater, Peter, praetor, skeeter, sweeter, tweeter; beefeater, Demeter, eggbeater, man-eater, repeater, saltpeter, smoke-eater; centime-

ter, decimeter, kilometer, lotus-eater, milli-
meter, overeater.
-eater (-ā-). See **-ator.**
-eather (-ē-), breather, either, neither, see-
ther, sheather, wreather.
-eather (-e-), blether, feather, heather,
leather, nether, tether, weather, wether,
whether; aweather, bellwether, pinfeather,
together, whitleather; altogether, get-
together.
-eathing, breathing, seething, sheathing,
teething, wreathing; bequeathing, fire-
breathing.
-eatly. See **-etely.**
-eaty, meaty, peaty, sleety, sweetie, sweety,
treaty, ziti; entreaty, Tahiti.
-eauty. See **-ooty.**
-eaven. See **-even.**
-eaver, beaver, cleaver, fever, griever,
keever, leaver, lever, reaver, riever,
weaver, weever; achiever, believer, con-
ceiver, deceiver, enfever, receiver; cantile-
ver, overachiever, unbeliever, under
achiever.
-eavy. See **-evy.**
-eazy. See **-easy.**
-ebble, pebble, rebel, treble.
-ebel. See **-ebble.**
-eber. See **-abor.**
-eble. See **-ebble.**
-ebo, gazebo, placebo.
-ebtor. See **-etter.**
-ecant, piquant, precant, secant; cosecant;
intersecant.
-ecca, Mecca; Rebecca.

-ecco. See **-echo.**

-ecent (-ē-), decent, puissant, recent; indecent, obeisant.

-echer. See **-etcher.**

-echo, echo, gecko, secco; art deco, El Greco, re-echo.

-ecian. See **-etion.**

-ecious, specious; capricious, facetious.

-ecis. See **-acy.**

-ecker, checker, chequer, pecker, trekker, wrecker; exchequer, woodpecker; double-decker, rubbernecker, triple-decker.

-eckle, deckle, freckle, heckle, keckle, Seckel, shekel, speckle; bespeckle; Dr. Jekyll.

-eckless, feckless, fleckless, necklace, reckless, speckless.

-ecko. See **-echo.**

-eckon, beckon, reckon, Schnecken.

-eco. See **-echo.**

-econd, beckoned, fecund, reckoned, second; nanosecond.

-ectant, expectant, reflectent; disinfectant.

-ectar. See **-ector.**

-ecter. See **-ector.**

-ectful, neglectful, respectful; disrespectful.

-ectic, hectic, pectic; cachectic, eclectic; analectic, anorectic, apoplectic, catalectic, dialectic.

-ectile, sectile; erectile, insectile, projectile.

-ection, flection, lection, section; affection, bisection, collection, complexion, confection, connection, convection, correction, defection, deflection, dejection, detection, direction, dissection, ejection, election, erection, infection, inflection, injection, inspection, midsection, objection, perfection, projection, protection, reflection, rejection, selection, subjection, subsection, trajection, trisection; circumspection, disaffection, disinfection, genuflexion, imperfection, indirection, insurrection, interjection, introspection, misdirection, predilection, preselection, recollection, re-election, resurrection, retrospection, venesection, vivisection.

-ective, affective, adjective, collective, connective, corrective, defective, deflective, detective, directive, effective, elective, erective, infective, inflective, injective, invective, neglective, objective, perfective, perspective, projective, prospective, protective, reflective, rejective, respective, selective, subjective; cost-effective, ineffective, introspective, irrespective, nonobjective, retrospective.

-ectly, abjectly, correctly, directly, erectly; incorrectly, indirectly.

-ector, flector, hector, Hector, lector, nectar, rector, sector, specter, vector; collector, convector, defector, deflector, detector, director, ejecter, elector, injecter, inspector, objector, projector, prospector, protector, reflector, selector.

-ecture, lecture, confecture, conjecture, prefecture, projecture; architecture.

-ecund. See **-econd.**

-edal (-e-). See **-eddle.**

-edal (-ē-). See **-eedle.**

-edden. See **-eaden.**

-edding, bedding, dreading, heading, lead-
ing, redding, shedding, shredding, sled-
ding, spreading, threading, wedding.

-eddle, heddle, medal, meddle, pedal, ped-
dle, reddle, treadle; backpedal, softpedal;
intermeddle.

-eddler, meddler, medlar, peddler, pedlar,
treadler.

-eddy, eddy, Freddy, heady, ready, steady,
Teddy; already, unready, unsteady.

-edence, credence, impedance, precedence;
antecedence, intercedence.

-edent, credent, needn't, sedent; decedent,
precedent, succedent; antecedent, interce-
dent.

-edger, dredger, edger, hedger, ledger,
pledger, sledger.

-edic, Vedic; comedic; orthopedic; encyclope-
dic.

-edit, credit, edit; accredit, discredit, mis-
credit; copyedit.

-edlar. See **-eddler.**

-edley. See **-eadly.**

-edo, credo, Lido; libido, toledo, Toledo, torpedo, tuxedo.

-eecher. See **-eacher.**

-eecy. See **-easy.**

-eedful, deedful, heedful, needful; unheed-
ful.

-eedle, beadle, needle, tweedle, wheedle.

-eedling, needling, reedling, seedling, twee-
dling, wheedling.

-eedy, beady, greedy, heedy, needy, reedy,
seedy, speedy, tweedy, weedy; indeedy.

-eefy, beefy, leafy, reefy.

-eekly. See **-eakly.**

-eely, eely, Ely, freely, Greeley, mealy, peely, really, squealy, steely; genteelly, surreally, scungilli, Swahili; campanile, touchy-feely.

-eeman, demon, freeman, leman, seaman, semen; Philemon; Lacedaemon.

-eemly. See **-emely.**

-eenly. See **-eanly.**

-eeny, beanie, genie, greeny, meanie, queenie, Sweeney, teeny, weenie, weeny; Alcmene, Athene, Bellini, bikini, Bikini, Cabrini, Cellini, Houdini, linguine, martini, Mycenae, Puccini, Rossini, tahini, zuc-chini; fettucine, Mussolini, scaloppine, spaghettini, Tetrazzini, tortellini.

-eepen, cheapen, deepen, steepen.

-eeper, beeper, cheaper, creeper, deeper, keeper, leaper, peeper, reaper, sleeper, steeper, sweeper, Ypres; beekeeper, book-keeper, doorkeeper, gatekeeper, house-keeper, innkeeper, peacekeeper, shop-keeper.

-eeple. See **-eople.**

-eeply, cheaply, deeply.
> Also: **-eep** + **-ly** (as in *steeply*, etc.)

-eepsie. See **-ypsy.**

-eepy, cheapie, creepy, sleepy, tepee, weepy.

-eerage, clearage, peerage, pierage, steerage; arrearage.

-eerful. See **-earful.**

-eerly. See **-erely.**

-eery. See **-eary.**

-eesi. See **-easy.**

-eesy. See **-easy.**

-eeten. See **-eaten.**

-eeter. See **-eater.**

-eether. See **-eather.**

-eetle, beetle, betel, fetal; decretal.

-eetly. See **-etely.**

-eety. See **-eaty.**

-eever. See **-eaver.**

-eevish, peevish, thievish.

-eezer. See **-easer.**

-eezing. See **-easing.**

-eezy. See **-easy.**

-egal, eagle, beagle, legal, regal; illegal, vice-regal; legal eagle, paralegal.

-eggar, beggar, egger; bootlegger, Heidegger.

-eggy, dreggy, eggy, leggy, Peggy.

-egian. See **-egion.**

-egion, legion, region; collegian, Glaswegian, Norwegian.

-egious. See **-igious.**

-egnant, pregnant, regnant; impregnant.

-egress, egress, regress.

-eifer. See **-ephyr.**

-eighbor. See **-abor.**

-einty. See **-ainty.**

-einy. See **-ainy.**

-eiress. See **-ris.**

-eisance. See **-ascence.**

-eist, deist, theist.

-eisure. See **-easure.**

-eiter. See **-itter.**

-either (-ī-). See **-ither.**

-either (-ē-). See **-eather.**

-eiver. See **-eaver.**

-ekyll. See **-eckle.**

-elate, helot, pellet, prelate, stellate, zealot; constellate; interpellate.

-elder, elder, gelder, melder, welder.

-elding, gelding, melding, welding.

-eldom, beldam, seldom.

-ele. See **-alely.**

-elee. See **-aylay.**

-elfish, elfish, pelfish, selfish, shellfish; unselfish.

-elic, bellic, melic, relic, telic; angelic; archangelic, evangelic, philatelic.

-eline, beeline, feline.

-elion, Pelion; aphelion, chameleon, Mendelian; perihelion.

-elix, Felix, helix.

-ella, Bella, Ella, fella, Stella; capella, Louella, patella, umbrella; Cinderella, Isabella, Pulcinella, tarantella.

-ellar. See **-eller.**

-ellas. See **-ealous.**

-ellen. See **-elon.**

-eller, cellar, dweller, feller, heller, seller, smeller, speller, stellar, teller; bestseller, expeller, foreteller, impeller, propeller, rathskeller, saltcellar; fortune teller, interstellar, Rockefeller, storyteller.

-ellet. See **-elate.**

-elli. See **-elly.**

-ellish, hellish, relish; embellish.

-ello, bellow, cello, felloe, fellow, hello, Jello, mellow, yellow; bedfellow, bordello, duello, good fellow, Longfellow, marshmallow, niello, Othello; brocatello, Donatello, Monticello, Pirandello, punchinello, saltarello; violoncello.

-ellous. See **-ealous.**

-ellow. See **-ello.**

-ellum, vellum; flagellum; antebellum, cerebellum.

-ellus. See **-ealous.**

-elly, belly, Delhi, deli, felly, jelly, Kelly, Nellie, Shelley, shelly, smelly, telly, wellie; cancelli, potbelly, rake-helly; Botticelli, Donatelli, vermicelli; Machiavelli.

-elon, Ellen, felon, Helen, melon; Magellan; watermelon.

-elop, develop, envelop.

-elot. See **-ellate.**

-elter, belter, felter, kelter, melter, pelter, shelter, smelter, spelter, swelter, welter; helter-skelter.

-elving, delving, helving, shelving.

-eman. See **-eeman.**

-ember, ember, member; December, dismember, November, remember, September; disremember.

-emble, semble, tremble; assemble, dissemble; reassemble.

-embly, trembly; assembly.

-emely, seemly; extremely, supremely, unseemly.

-emer. See **-eamer.**

-emic (-em-), chemic; alchemic, endemic, pandemic, polemic, systemic, totemic; academic, epidemic, theoremic.

-emic (-ē-), anemic, graphemic, morphemic, phonemic, taxemic.

-emish, blemish, Flemish.

-emlin, gremlin, Kremlin.

-emma, Emma, gemma; dilemma.

-emner. See **-emor.**

-emon. See **-eeman.**

-emor, hemmer, tremor; condemner, contemner.

-emplar, templar; exemplar.

-empter, tempter, attempter, exempter, preempter.

-emption, emption; ademption, coemption, exemption, pre-emption, redemption.

-emur. See **-eamer.**

-ena. See **-ina.**

-enace. See **-ennis.**

-enal, penal, renal, venal; adrenal, machinal.

-enant, pennant, tenant; lieutenant.

-enate. See **-ennet.**

-encer. See **-enser.**

-encher, bencher, blencher, censure, clencher, denture, quencher, trencher, venture, wencher; adventure, debenture, indenture; misadventure, peradventure.

-enchman, Frenchman, henchman.

-encil, mensal, pencil, pensil, pensile, stencil, tensile; extensile, prehensile, utensil.

-enda, Brenda, Zenda; addenda, agenda, credenda; corrigenda, hacienda.

-endance. See **-endence.**

-endant. See **-endent.**

-endence, tendance; ascendance, attendance, dependence, resplendence, transcendence; condescendence, independence; interdependence.

-endent, pendant, pendent, splendent; appendant, ascendant, attendant, contendent,

defendant, dependant, dependent, descend-
ant, descendent, impendent, intendant, re-
splendent, transcendent, transplendent; in-
dependent; interdependent, superintendent.

-ender, bender, blender, fender, gender,
lender, render, sender, slender, spender,
splendor, tender, vendor; amender, as-
cender, bartender, contender, defender,
emender, engender, extender, offender,
pretender, surrender, suspender, week-
ender; moneylender.

-ending, ending, pending.
    Also: **-end** + **-ing** (as in *ascending*,
    etc.)

-endor. See **-ender.**

-endous, horrendous, stupendous, tremen-
dous.

-endum, addendum, agendum, credendum,
pudendum; corrigendum, referendum.

-enely. See **-eanly.**

-enet. See **-ennet.**

-engthen, lengthen, strengthen.

-enial, genial, menial, venial; congenial.

-enic (-e-), phrenic; arsenic, Edenic, eugenic,
Hellenic, hygienic, irenic; allergenic, calis-
thenic, neurasthenic, Panhellenic, patho-
genic, photogenic, psychogenic, schizo-
phrenic, telegenic; carcinogenic;
hallucinogenic.

-enic (-ē-), scenic, splenic; Hellenic, hygienic,
irenic; Panhellenic.

-enie. See **-ainy.**

-enim. See **-enum.**

-enin. See **-enon.**

-enish, plenish, Rhenish, wennish; replenish.

-enna, henna, senna; antenna, duenna, Gehenna, Ravenna, Siena, sienna, Vienna.

-ennant. See **-enant.**

-ennel, fennel, kennel, antennal.

-enner. See **-enor.**

-ennet, Bennett, jennet, rennet, senate, tenet.

-ennis, Dennis, menace, tenace, tennis, Venice.

-enny, any, Benny, Denny, fenny, jenny, Jenny, Kenny, Lenny, many, penny, Kilkenny.

-eno, Reno, Zeno; bambino, casino, merino; Filipino, maraschino.

-enom. See **-enum.**

-enon, Lenin, pennon, tenon.

-enor, penner, tenor, tenour; countertenor, heldentenor.

-enser, censer, censor, denser, fencer, Spencer, Spenser, tensor; commencer, condenser, dispenser, extensor, intenser.

-ensil. See **-encil.**

-ensile. See **-encil.**

-ension. See **-ention.**

-ensive, pensive, tensive; ascensive, defensive, distensive, expensive, extensive, intensive, offensive, ostensive, protensive, suspensive, apprehensive, comprehensive, hypertensive, indefensive, inexpensive, inoffensive, reprehensive; incomprehensive; labor-intensive.

-ensor. See **-enser.**

-enta, yenta; magenta, placenta, polenta; impedimenta.

-ental, cental, dental, gentle, lentil, mental,

rental; fragmental, parental, pigmental, placental, segmental, tridental, accidental, alimental, complemental, complimental, continental, departmental, detrimental, elemental, fundamental, governmental, incidental, instrumental, ligamental, monumental, occidental, oriental, ornamental, regimental, rudimental, sacramental, supplemental, testamental, transcendental; coincidental, developmental, experimental, impedimental, temperamental, transcontinental; intercontinental.

-entance, sentence, repentance; unrepentance.

-entence. See **-entance.**

-enter, center, enter, mentor, renter, tenter; dissenter, frequenter, inventor, lamenter, off-center, precentor, presenter, re-enter, repenter, tormentor; epicenter, ornamenter; experimenter.

-entful, eventful, repentful, resentful; uneventful.

-ential, agential, credential, essential, potential, prudential, sentential, sequential, tangential, torrential; confidential, consequential, deferential, differential, evidential, existential, exponential, inferential, influential, penitential, pestilential, precedential, preferential, presidential, providential, quintessential, referential, reverential, unessential; circumferential, equipotential, experiential, inconsequential.

-entic, authentic, identic.

-entil. See **-ental.**

-entile, gentile; percentile.

-entin, dentin, Lenten, Trenton; San Quentin.

-enting, denting, renting, scenting, tenting, venting; absenting, accenting, assenting, augmenting, cementing, consenting, fermenting, fomenting, frequenting, lamenting, presenting, preventing, relenting, resenting, tormenting; circumventing, complimenting, ornamenting, representing, supplementing; misrepresenting.

-ention, gentian, mention, pension, tension; abstention, ascension, attention, contention, convention, declension, detention, dimension, dissension, distension, extension, intention, invention, pretension, prevention, propension, recension, retention, suspension; apprehension, circumvention, comprehension, condescension, contravention, inattention, intervention, reprehension; incomprehension, misapprehension.

-entious, abstentious, contentious, dissentious, licentious, pretentious, sententious, silentious; tendentious, conscientious, pestilentious, unpretentious.

-entist, dentist, prenticed; Adventist, apprenticed, preventist.

-entive, assentive, attentive, incentive, presentive, retentive; disincentive, inattentive.

-entle. See **-ental.**

-entment, contentment, presentment, relentment, resentment; discontentment.

-ento, cento, lento; memento, pimento; Sacramento; divertimento.

-entor (-ôr-), centaur, mentor, stentor; succentor.

-entor (-ər-), See **-enter.**

-entous, apprentice, momentous, portentous; compos mentis; non compos mentis; in loco parentis.

-entric, centric; acentric, concentric, eccentric, geocentric; anthropocentric, heliocentric.

-entry, entry, gentry, sentry.

-enture. See **-encher.**

-enty, al dente, plenty, scenty, twenty; aplenty, cognoscenti, licenti; twenty-twenty; Deo Volente; Agua Caliente, dolce far niente.

-enu, menu, venue.

-enum, denim, frenum, plenum, venom.

-eny. See **-ainy.**

-enza, cadenza, credenza; influenza.

-eo, Cleo, Leo, Rio, trio; radio, stereo.

-eomen. See **-omen.**

-eon, aeon, Creon, Leon, neon, paean, peon; pantheon; Anacreon.

-eopard, jeopard, leopard, peppered, shepherd.

-eople, people, steeple; unpeople.

-epee. See **-eepy.**

-epherd. See **-eopard.**

-ephyr, deafer, feoffor, heifer, zephyr.

-epid, tepid, trepid; intrepid.

-epper, leper, pepper, stepper; high-stepper.

-epsy, catalepsy, epilepsy.

-eptic, peptic, septic, skeptic; aseptic, dispeptic, eupeptic; antiseptic, cataleptic, epileptic.

-era, era, Hera, lira, Madeira, Vera; chimera; Halmahera.

-erance. See **-earance.**

-ercer. See **-urser.**

-ercion. See **-ertion.**

-erder. See **-urder.**

-erdure. See **-erger.**

-erely, cheerly, clearly, dearly, merely, nearly, queerly, sheerly, yearly; austerely, severely, sincerely; cavalierly, insincerely.

-erence. See **-earance.**

-ergeant. See **-argent.**

-ergence, convergence, divergence, emergence, resurgence, submergence.

-ergent, turgent, urgent, vergent; abstergent, assurgent, convergent, detergent, divergent, emergent, insurgent, resurgent.

-erger, merger, perjure, purger, scourger, splurger, urger, verdure, verger; converger, diverger, emerger, submerger.

-ergy. See **-urgy.**

-eri. See **-erry.**

-eric, cleric, Derek, derrick, Eric, ferric, Herrick, spheric; chimeric, enteric, generic, Homeric, hysteric, mesmeric, numeric, atmospheric, chromospheric, climacteric, esoteric, exoteric, hemispheric, isomeric, neoteric, peripheric, phylacteric.

-eries, dearies, queries, series, wearies.

-eril, beryl, Cheryl, feral, Merrill, Meryl, peril, sterile. See also **-erule.**

-erile. See **-eril.**

-erish, cherish, perish.

-erit, ferret, merit; demerit, inherit; disinherit.

-erjure. See **-erger.**

-erker. See **-irker.**

-erkin, firkin, gherkin, jerkin, merkin, Perkin.

-erky, jerky, murky, perky, turkey.

-erling. See **-urling.**

-erly. See **-urly.**

-ermal, dermal, thermal.

-erman, Berman, Burman, ermine, firman, German, Herman, merman, sermon, Sherman, Thurman; determine, Mount Hermon; predetermine.

-erment, ferment; affirmant, averment, conferment, deferment, determent, interment, preferment, referment; disinterment.

-ermes, Burmese, Hermes, kermes.

-ermine. See **-erman.**

-ermy, fermi, germy, Nurmi, squirmy, wormy; diathermy, taxidermy.

-ernal, colonel, journal, kernel, sternal, urnal, vernal; cavernal, diurnal, eternal, external, fraternal, hibernal, infernal, internal, maternal, nocturnal, paternal, supernal; co-eternal, sempiternal.

-ernest. See **-earnest.**

-erning. See **-earning.**

-ernist. See **-earnest.**

-ero (-ē-), hero, Nero, zero.

-ero (-â-). See **-aro.**

-errand, errand, gerund.

-errant, errant; aberrant, knight-errant.

-errick. See **-eric.**

-errier, burier, merrier, terrier.

-erring, derring, erring, herring.

-erry, berry, bury, cherry, Derry, ferry, Jerry, Kerry, merry, Perry, sherry, skerry, Terry, very, wherry; Bambury, blackberry, blueberry, cranberry, gooseberry, mulberry, raspberry, strawberry; beriberi, boysenberry, capillary, cemetery, culinary, elderberry, huckleberry, Janissary, lamasery, loganberry, millinery, monastery, Pondicherry, presbytery, stationary, stationery. See also **-ary.**

-ersal, bursal, tercel, versal; rehearsal, reversal, transversal; universal.

-ersey, furzy, jersey, Jersey, kersey.

-ersian. See **-ersion.**

-ersion, Persian, version; aspersion, aversion, conversion, discursion, dispersion, diversion, excursion, immersion, incursion, inversion, perversion, reversion, submersion, subversion; extroversion, introversion; animadversion.

-erson, person, worsen.

-ertain, Burton, certain, curtain, Merton; uncertain.

-erter, blurter, curter, flirter, hurter, squirter; asserter, averter, converter, deserter, diverter, inserter, inverter, perverter, subverter.

-ertie. See **-irty.**

-ertile. See **-urtle.**

-ertion, tertian; assertion, Cistercian, coercion, desertion, exertion, insertion; self-assertion.

-ertive, furtive; assertive, divertive, exertive, revertive.

-ertly, curtly, pertly; alertly, expertly; inertly, invertly, overtly; inexpertly.

-erule, ferule, ferrule. See also **-eril.**

-ervant, fervent, servant; conservant, observant, recurvant; unobservant.

-ervent. See **-ervant.**

-erver, fervor, server, swerver; conserver, observer, preserver, reserver, time-server.

-ervy. See **-urvy.**

-ery. See **-erry.**

-escence, essence; candescence, excresence, fluorescence, pubescence, putrescence, quiescence, quintessence, senescence, tumescence; acquiescence, adolescence, coalescence, convalescence, deliquescence, effervescence, efflorescence, evanescence, incandescence, iridescence, obsolescence, opalescence, phosphorescence, recrudescence; preadolescence.

-escent (-es-), cessant, crescent, jessant; candescent, depressant, excresent, fluorescent, ignescent, incessant, liquescent, putrescent, quiescent, rubescent, senescent; adolescent, convalescent, deliquescent, detumescent, effervescent, efflorescent, evanescent, incandescent, luminescent, obsolescent, opalescent, phosphorescent, recrudescent; antidepressant.

-escience, nescience, prescience.

-escue, fescue, rescue; Montesquieu.

-esence, pleasance, presence; omnipresence. Also: **-easant** + **-s** (as in *peasants,* etc.)

-esent. See **-easant.**

-eshen. See **-ession.**

-esher, fresher, pressure, thresher; refresher.

-eshly, fleshly, freshly; specially; especially.

-esian. See **-esion.**

-esion, Frisian, lesion; adhesion, artesian, Cartesian, cohesion, Ephesian, Parisian, Silesian; Indonesian, Micronesian, Polynesian.

-esis, Croesus, rhesus, thesis; mimesis, prothesis; anamnesis, catachresis, exegesis; hyperkinesis, Peloponnesus, telekinesis; amniocentesis, aposiopesis.

-essage, message, presage; expressage.

-essal. See **-estle.**

-essant. See **-escent.**

-essel. See **-estle.**

-essence. See **-escence.**

-esser. See **-essor.**

-essful, stressful; distressful, successful; unsuccessful.

-essie. See **-essy.**

-essing, blessing, dressing, guessing, pressing.

Also: **-ess** + **-ing** (as in *depressing*, etc.)

Also: **-esce** + **-ing** (as in *convalescing*, etc.)

-ession, cession, freshen, Hessian, session; accession, aggression, bull session, compression, concession, confession, depression, digression, discretion, expression, impression, ingression, obsession, oppression, possession, precession, procession, profession, progression, recession, secession, succession, suppression, transgression; decompression, indiscretion, intercession, prepossession, dispossession, repossession, retrocession, retrogression, self-expression, self-possession, supersession.

-essive, aggressive, compressive, concessive, depressive, digressive, excessive, expressive, impressive, obsessive, oppressive, possessive, progressive, recessive, regressive, repressive, successive, suppressive, transgressive; retrogressive; manic-depressive.

-essor, dresser, guesser, lesser, lessor, presser; addresser, aggressor, assessor, compressor, confessor, depressor, oppressor, possessor, professor, successor, suppressor, transgressor; antecessor, intercessor, predecessor, second-guesser, tongue-depressor.

-essure. See **-esher.**

-essy, Bessie, dressy, Jesse, Jessie, messy, Tessie.

-esta, Vesta; celesta, fiesta, siesta.

-estal, festal, vestal.

-ester, Chester, ester, Esther, fester, Hester, jester, Leicester, Lester, Nestor, pester, tester, vester, wrester; Chichester, Colchester, digester, Dorchester, Eastchester, investor, Manchester, nor'wester, protester, Rochester, semester, sequester, sou'wester, Sylvester, trimester, Westchester; empty-nester, polyester.

-estial, bestial; celestial.

-estic, domestic, majestic; anapestic, catachrestic.

-estine, destine; clandestine, intestine, predestine.

-estive, festive, restive; attestive, congestive, digestive, suggestive, tempestive.

-estle, Cecil, nestle, pestle, trestle, vessel, wrestle.

-esto, pesto, presto; manifesto.

-estral, kestrel; ancestral, fenestral, orchestral, trimestral.

-esture, gesture; divesture, investure.

-esty, chesty, cresty, resty, testy, zesty.

-esus. See **-esis.**

-etal. See **-ettle.**

-etcher, etcher, fetcher, fletcher, kvetcher, lecher, retcher, sketcher, stretcher.

-etchy, sketchy, stretchy, tetchy.

-ete. See **-etty.**

-etely, fleetly, meetly, neatly, sweetly; completely, concretely, discreetly; incompletely, indiscreetly, obsoletely.

-eter. See **-eater.**

-ethel, Bethel, Ethel, ethyl, methyl.

-ether. See **-eather.**

-ethyl. See **-ethel.**

-etic, aesthetic, ascetic, athletic, balletic, bathetic, cosmetic, emetic, frenetic, genetic, hermetic, kinetic, magnetic, mimetic, pathetic, phonetic, phrenetic, poetic, prophetic, splenetic, synthetic; alphabetic, analgetic, anaesthetic, antithetic, apathetic, arithmetic, dietetic, energetic, exegetic, geodetic, homiletic, hypothetic, masoretic, parenthetic, sympathetic, theoretic; antipathetic, biogenetic, peripatetic; cyanogetic; unapologetic; onomatopoetic.

-etion (-ē-), Grecian; accretion, completion, concretion, deletion, depletion, excretion,

Phoenician, repletion, secretion, Tahitian;
Polynesian.
- **-etion** (-e-). See **-ession.**
- **-etious.** See **-ecious.**
- **-etish.** See **-ettish.**
- **-eto,** Tito, veto; bonito, Hirohito, mosquito;
  incognito.
- **-etor.** See **-etter.**
- **-etter,** better, bettor, debtor, fetter, getter,
  letter, setter, wetter, whetter; abettor, be-
  getter, forgetter, go-getter, newsletter,
  pacesetter, red-letter, typesetter, unfetter.
- **-etti.** See **-etty.**
- **-ettish,** fetish, Lettish, pettish, wettish; co-
  quettish.
- **-ettle,** fettle, Gretel, kettle, metal, mettle,
  nettle, petal, settle; abettal, unsettle; Popo-
  catapetl.
- **-etto,** ghetto, petto; falsetto, libretto, pal-
  metto, stiletto, terzetto, zuchetto; alle-
  gretto, lazaretto, Rigoletto; Tintoretto.
- **-ettor.** See **-etter.**
- **-etty** (-e-), Betty, fretty, Hetty, jetty, Lettie,
  netty, petit, petty, sweaty; confetti, libretti,
  machete, Rossetti, spaghetti; Donizetti,
  spermaceti.
- **-etty** (-i-). See **-itty.**
- **-etus,** fetus, Thetis, treatise; boletus, coitus,
  quietus.
- **-euced.** See **-ucid.**
- **-eudal.** See **-oodle.**
- **-eudo.** See **-udo.**
- **-eum,** lyceum, museum, no-see-um, per
  diem, Te Deum; atheneum, colosseum,
  mausoleum; peritoneum.

-eura. See **-ura.**

-eural. See **-ural.**

-euter. See **-ooter.**

-eutic, scorbutic; hermaneutic, pharmaceutic, therapeutic.

-eutist. See **-utist.**

-eval. See **-evil.**

-evel, bevel, devil, level, Neville, revel; bedevil, dishevel.

-even (-e-), Devon, heaven, leaven, seven; eleven.

-even (-ē-), even, Stephen, Steven; uneven.

-ever (-e-), clever, ever, lever, never, sever, Trevor; assever, dissever, endeavor, however, whatever, whenever, wherever, whichever, whoever, whomever; howsoever, whatsoever, whencesoever, wheresoever, whomsoever, whosoever.

-ever (-ē-). See **-eaver.**

-evil (-ē-), evil, weevil; coeval, primeval, retrieval, upheaval; medieval.

-evil (-e-). See **-evel.**

-evious, devious, previous.

-evy, bevy, Chevy, heavy, levee, levy; topheavy.

-ewal. See **-uel.**

-eward, leeward, sewered, skewered, steward.

-ewdest. See **-udist.**

-ewdish. See **-udish.**

-ewdly. See **-udely.**

-ewel. See **-uel.**

-ewer, brewer, ewer, fewer, hewer, sewer, viewer.

-ewish, blueish, Jewish, newish, shrewish.

-ewly. See **-uly.**

-ewry. See **-ury.**

-ewsy. See **-oozy.**

-ewy, bluey, buoy, chewy, cooee, dewy, Dewey, fluey, gluey, gooey, hooey, Louie, Louis, pfui, screwy; chop suey; ratatouille.

-exas. See **-exus.**

-exer, flexor, vexer; annexer, perplexer.

-exile, exile, flexile.

-extant, extant, sextant.

-extile, sextile, textile; bissextile.

-exus, nexus, plexus, Texas; Alexis; solar plexus.

-exy, prexy, sexy; apoplexy.

-eyance, abeyance, conveyance, purveyance.

-eyor. See **-ayer.**

-eyrie. See **-ary.**

-ezi. See **-easy.**

-ia. See **-ea.**

-iad, dryad, naiad, triad; jeremiad.

-ial, dial, phial, trial, vial, viol; decrial, denial, espial, mistrial, retrial, sundial, supplial.

-iam, Priam, Siam; Omar Khayyam.

-ian. See **-ion.**

-iance, clients, giants, science; affiance, alliance, appliance, compliance, defiance, reliance, suppliance; misalliance.

-iant, client, giant, pliant, scient; affiant, compliant, defiant, reliant.

-iants. See **-iance.**

-iaper. See **-iper.**

-iar. See **-ier.**

-iary. See **-iry.**

-ias, bias, pious; Elias, Tobias; Ananias, nisi prius.

-iat. See **-iet.**

-ibal. See **-ible.**

-ibald. See **-ibbled.**

-ibber, bibber, cribber, dibber, fibber, gibber, glibber, jibber, squibber; ad-libber, wine-bibber.

-ibbet. See **-ibit.**

-ibble, cribble, dibble, dribble, fribble, kibble, nibble, quibble, scribble, sibyl, Sybil, thribble; ish-kabibble.

-ibbled, dibbled, dribbled, kibbled, nibbled, piebald, quibbled, ribald, scribbled.

-ibbling, dibbling, dribbling, nibbling, quibbling, scribbling, sibling.

-ibbly, dribbly, fribbly, glibly, nibbly, quibbly, scribbly, tribbly.

-ibbon, gibbon, ribbon.

-ibel. See **-ible.**

-iber, briber, fiber, giber, Tiber; imbiber, inscriber, prescriber, subscriber, transcriber.

-ibit, gibbet, Tibbett, zibet; exhibit, inhibit, prohibit.

-ible, Bible, libel, tribal.

-iblet, driblet, giblet, triblet.

-ibling. See **-ibbling.**

-ibyl. See **-ibble.**

-ica, mica, Micah, pica.

-icar. See **-icker.**

-icely. See **-isely.**

-icial, comitial, initial, judicial, official; artifi-

cial, beneficial, interstitial, prejudicial, sac-
rificial, superficial.

-ician. See **-ition.**

-icient, deficient, efficient, omniscient, profi-
cient, sufficient; coefficient, inefficient, in-
sufficient.

-icious, vicious; ambitious, auspicious, capricious, delicious, factitious, fictitious, judi-
cious, lubricious, malicious, Mauritius, nu-
tritious, officious, pernicious, propitious,
seditious, suspicious; adventitious, avari-
cious, expeditious, inauspicious, injudi-
cious, meretricious, superstitious, supposi-
tious, surreptitious.

-icken, chicken, quicken, sicken, stricken,
thicken, wicken; awestricken; panic-
stricken.

-icker, bicker, dicker, flicker, kicker, knicker,
licker, liquor, picker, quicker, sicker,
slicker, snicker, thicker, ticker, vicar,
wicker; bootlicker, nitpicker.

-icket, clicket, cricket, picket, piquet, pricket,
thicket, ticket, wicket.

-ickle, chicle, fickle, mickle, nickel, pickle,
prickle, sickle, stickle, strickle, tickle,
trickle; bicycle, icicle, vehicle; pumper-
nickel.

-ickly, prickly, quickly, sickly, slickly,
thickly, trickly.

-ickset, quickset, thickset.

-ickshaw, kickshaw, rickshaw.

-icky, dickey, Dicky, Mickey, Nicky, quickie,
rickey, sticky, tricky, Vicki.

-icle. See **-ickle.**

-icon. See **-iken.**

-icter, lictor, stricter, victor; afflicter, conflicter, constrictor, inflicter, predicter; contradicter; boa constrictor, vasoconstrictor.

-iction, diction, fiction, friction; addiction, affliction, confliction, constriction, conviction, depiction, eviction, infliction, nonfiction, prediction, reliction, restriction, transfixion; benediction, contradiction, dereliction, interdiction, jurisdiction, malediction, metafiction, valediction.

-ictive, fictive; afflictive, conflictive, constrictive, inflictive, predictive, restrictive, vindictive; benedictive, contradictive, interdictive, jurisdictive.

-ictor. See **-icter.**

-ictualler. See **-ittler.**

-icture, picture, stricture; depicture.

-icy, icy, spicy.

-idal, bridal, bridle, idle, idol, idyll, sidle, tidal; fratricidal, germicidal, herbicidal, homicidal, matricidal, parricidal, regicidal, suicidal; infanticidal, insecticidal, tyrannicidal.

-idden, bidden, chidden, hidden, midden, ridden, stridden; bedridden, forbidden, unbidden.

-iddle, diddle, fiddle, griddle, piddle, quiddle, riddle, tiddle, twiddle.

-iddling, fiddling, kidling, middling, piddling, riddling, twiddling.

-iddy, biddy, giddy, kiddie, middy, midi, stiddy.

-iden, guidon, Haydn, Leyden, widen; Poseidon.

-ident, bident, rident, strident, trident.

-ider, cider, eider, glider, guider, hider, rider, spider, wider; backslider, confider, divider, insider, outrider, outsider, provider.

-idget, Bridget, digit, fidget, midget.

-idgy, midgy, ridgy.

-idle. See **-idal.**

-idly, idly, widely.

-idney, kidney, Sidney.

-ido. See **-edo.**

-idol. See **-idal.**

-idy, Friday, Heidi, tidy; untidy; bona fide.

-idyl. See **-idal.**

-iefly, briefly, chiefly.

-ience. See **-iance.**

-ient. See **-iant.**

-ients. See **-iance.**

-ier, briar, buyer, drier, dyer, flier, friar, fryer, higher, liar, mire, nigher, plier, prior, pryer, shyer, slyer, spryer, spyer, Tyre, vier.
   Also: **-y** + **-er** (as in *amplifier,* etc.) See also: **-ire.**

-iery. See **-iry.**

-iestly. See **-eastly.**

-iet, diet, fiat, quiet, riot, striate; disquiet.

-ieval. See **-evil.**

-iever. See **-eaver.**

-ifer, cipher, fifer, knifer, lifer, rifer; decipher.

-iffin, biffin, griffin, griffon, stiffen.

-iffle, piffle, riffle, sniffle, whiffle.

-iffy, iffy, jiffy, sniffy, spiffy.

-ific, glyphic; deific, horrific, pacific, pontific, prolific, somnific, specific, terrific; beatific, calorific, hieroglyphic, honorific, humorific, scientific, soporific.

-ifle, Eiffel, eyeful, rifle, stifle, trifle.

-ifling, rifling, stifling, trifling.

-ifter, drifter, grifter, lifter, shifter, sifter, swifter; shoplifter, uplifter.

-iftless, driftless, shiftless, thriftless.

-ifty, drifty, fifty, nifty, rifty, shifty, thrifty.

-igate. See **-igot.**

-iggard. See **-iggered.**

-igger, bigger, chigger, digger, jigger, rigger, rigor, swigger, trigger, twigger, vigor; gold digger, grave digger, outrigger.

-iggered, figgered, jiggered, niggard.

-iggle, giggle, higgle, jiggle, niggle, sniggle, squiggle, wiggle, wriggle.

-igher. See **-ier.**

-ighland. See **-island.**

-ighly. See **-ily.**

-ighness. See **-inus.**

-ighten, brighten, Brighton, frighten, heighten, lighten, tighten, Titan, triton, whiten; enlighten.

-ightening, brightening, frightening, lightning, tightening, whitening.

-ighter, biter, blighter, brighter, fighter, kiter, lighter, miter, niter, tighter, titer, triter, writer; backbiter, first-nighter, igniter, inciter, inditer, moonlighter, speechwriter, prize fighter, typewriter; copywriter, dynamiter, underwriter.

-ightful, frightful, mightful, rightful, spiteful, sprightful; delightful, insightful.

-ighting. See **-iting.**

-ightly, brightly, knightly, lightly, nightly, sprightly, tightly, tritely; politely, unsightly; impolitely.

-ightning. See **-ightening.**

-ighty, blighty, flighty, mighty, mitey, nightie, whitey; almighty; Aphrodite.

-igil, sigil, strigil, vigil.

-igious, litigious, prodigious, religious; irreligious, sacrilegious.

-igit. See **-idget.**

-igly. See **-iggly.**

-igma, sigma, stigma; enigma.

-igment, figment, pigment.

-ignant, benignant, indignant, malignant.

-igner. See **-iner.**

-ignly. See **-inely.**

-ignment, alignment, assignment, confinement, consignment, designment, entwinement, inclinement, refinement, resignment.

-igor. See **-igger.**

-igot, bigot, frigate, gigot, spigot.

-iguer. See **-eager.**

-iken, icon, lichen, liken.

-iking, biking, diking, hiking, liking, piking, spiking, striking, Viking; disliking.

-ila. See **-illa.**

-ilbert, filbert, Gilbert.

-ilding. See **-uilding.**

-ildish, childish, mildish, wildish.

-ildly, childly, mildly, wildly.

-ildor. See **-uilder.**

-ile. See **-illy.**

-ilely. See **-ily.**

-ili. See **-illy.**

-ilian. See **-illion.**

-ilient. See **-illiant.**

-ilight, highlight, skylight, twilight.

-ilious, bilious; punctilious; atrabilious, supercilious.

-ilken, milken, silken.

-ilky, milky, silky, Wilkie.

-illa, Scylla, villa, Willa; ancilla, Attila, axilla, Camilla, cedilla, chinchilla, flotilla, gorilla, guerrilla, manila, Manila, mantilla, megillah, Priscilla, vanilla; camarilla, cascarilla, sabadilla, sarsaparilla.

-illage, grillage, pillage, tillage, village.

-iller, chiller, driller, filler, griller, killer, miller, pillar, Schiller, spiller, swiller, thriller, tiller; distiller, maxillar; caterpillar, ladykiller.

-illes. See **-illies.**

-illet, billet, fillet, millet, rillet, skillet.

-illful, skillful, willful; unskillful.

-illian. See **-illion.**

-illiant, brilliant; resilient.

-illiard, billiard, milliard, mill-yard.

-illie. See **-illy.**

-illie. See **-illy.**

-illies, fillies, gillies, lilies, willies; Achilles, Antilles.

-illing, billing, shilling, willing; unwilling. Also: **-ill** + **-ing** (as in *filling,* etc.)

-illion, billion, Lillian, jillion, million, pillion, trillion, zillion; Castilian, civilian, cotillion, gazillion, pavilion, postilion, quadrillion, Quintilian, quintillion, reptilian, vermilion; crocodilian, Maximilian.

-illo. See **-illow.**

-illow, billow, pillow, willow; Negrillo; armadillo, cigarillo, peccadillo.

-illy, billy, Billy, Chile, chili, chilly, filly, frilly, gillie, grilly, hilly, lily, Lily, Millie, Scilly, shrilly, silly, stilly, Tillie, Willie; bacilli, Caerphilly, daylilly, fusilli; Piccadilly, piccalilli, tiger lily, water lily, willy-nilly; daffy-down-dilly.

-ilo. See **-illow.**

-ilot, eyelet, islet, pilot.

-ilter, filter, jilter, kilter, milter, philter, quilter.

-ilton, Hilton, Milton, Stilton, Wilton.

-ily (-ī-), drily, highly, Reilly, Riley, shyly, slyly, smiley, wily, wryly; O'Reilly.

-ily (-i-). See **-illy.**

-image, image, scrimmage.

-imate, climate, primate; acclimate.

-imber, limber, timber, timbre; unlimber.

-imble, cymbal, fimble, Gimbel, nimble, symbol, thimble, tymbal, wimble.

-imbo, bimbo, limbo; akimbo.

-imely, primely, timely; sublimely, untimely.

-imen. See **-imon.**

-imer. See **-immer.**

-imey. See **-imy.**

-imic, gimmick, mimic; alchymic, cherubimic, eponymic, homonymic, matronymic, metonymic, pantomimic, patronymic, synonymic.

-iming, chiming, climbing, liming, priming, rhyming, timing.

-imly, dimly, grimly, primly, trimly.

-immer, brimmer, dimmer, glimmer, grim-
mer, primer, primmer, shimmer, simmer,
skimmer, slimmer, swimmer, trimmer.

-imming, brimming, dimming, skimming,
slimming, swimming, trimming.

-immy, gimme, jimmy, Jimmy, shimmy.

-imon, Hyman, Hymen, limen, Lyman, pie-
man, Simon.

-imper, crimper, limper, scrimper, shrimper,
simper, whimper.

-imple, crimple, dimple, pimple, rimple, simple, wimple.

-imply, crimply, dimply, limply, pimply, sim-
ply.

-impy, impy, scrimpy.

-imsy, flimsy, mimsy, slimsy, whimsy, Wim-
sey.

-imy, blimey, grimy, limey, limy, rimy,
slimy, stymie, thymy.

-ina (-ē-), Deena, Gina, Lena, Nina, scena,
Tina; arena, Athena, cantina, catena,
Christina, czarina, Edwina, farina, galena,
Georgina, Helena, hyena, Katrina, Marina,
Medina, Messina, patina, Regina, retsina,
Rowena, subpoena, tsarina, verbena; Ange-
lina, Argentina, ballerina, Catalina, cava-
tina, concertina, ocarina, Palestrina, Pasa-
dena, philopena, scarlatina, semolina,
signorina, Wilhelmina; Herzegovina, Pallas
Athena.

-ina (-ī-), china, China, Dinah, Heine, Ina,
myna; Regina; Carolina.

-inal, binal, crinal, final, spinal, trinal, vinyl;
acclinal, caninal, equinal, piscinal; anticli-
nal, officinal, semifinal.

-inas. See **-inus.**

-inca, Inca, vinca; Katrinka.

-incher, clincher, flincher, lyncher, pincher;
penny-pincher; Doberman pinscher.

-inctly, distinctly, succinctly; indistinctly.

-incture, cincture, tincture; encincture.

-inder, cinder, flinder, tinder; rescinder.

-indle, brindle, dwindle, kindle, spindle,
swindle; enkindle, rekindle.

-indly, blindly, kindly; unkindly.

-indy, Hindi, Lindy, shindy, windy.

-inea. See **-inny.**

-inear. See **-innier.**

-inely, finely; benignly, caninely, divinely,
supinely; saturninely.

-inement. See **-ignment.**

-iner, diner, finer, liner, miner, minor,
shiner, Shriner, signer, whiner; airliner, as-
signer, consignor, definer, designer, eye-
liner, hardliner, jetliner, one-liner, recliner,
refiner; Asia Minor, forty-niner, party-liner,
Ursa Minor.

-inet. See **-innet.**

-inew. See **-inue.**

-iney. See **-iny.**

-inful, sinful, skinful.

-ingent, stringent; astringent, constringent,
contingent, restringent.

-inger (-in-jər), cringer, fringer, ginger,
hinger, injure, singer, twinger; infringer.

-inger (-ing-ər), bringer, flinger, ringer,
singer, slinger, springer, stinger, stringer,
wringer; folksinger, gunslinger, humdinger,

leftwinger, mudslinger, rightwinger; Meistersinger, minnesinger.

-inger (-ing-gər), finger, linger; malinger.

-ingle, cingle, cringle, dingle, ingle, jingle, mingle, shingle, single, swingle, tingle, tringle; commingle, Kris Kringle, surcingle; intermingle.

-ingly, jingly, mingly, shingly, singly, tingly.

-ingo, bingo, dingo, gringo, jingo, lingo; Domingo, flamingo.

-ingy (-ing-ē), clingy, dinghy, springy, stingy, stringy, swingy, zingy.

-ingy (-in-jē), cringy, dingy, fringy, stingy, swingy, twingy.

-ini. See **-eeny.**

-inian. See **-inion.**

-inic, clinic, cynic; actinic, aclinic, delphinic, fulminic, platinic, rabbinic, Jacobinic, narcotinic, nicotinic, polygynic.

-ining, dining, lining.

Also: **-ine** + **-ing** (as in *mining*, etc.)
Also: **-ign** + **-ing** (as in *signing*, etc.)

-inion, minion, pinion, piñon; Darwinian, dominion, opinion, Virginian; Abyssinian, Augustinian, Carolinian, Carthaginian, Palestinian.

-inish (-in-), finish, Finnish, thinnish, tinnish; diminish, refinish.

-inish (-ī-), brinish, swinish.

-inist, plenist; machinist, routinist; magazinist.

Also: **-ean** + **-est** (as in *cleanest*, etc.)
Also: **-een** + **-est** (as in *greenest*, etc.)

-injure. See **-inger.**

-inker, blinker, clinker, drinker, inker,

shrinker, sinker, slinker, stinker, thinker, tinker, winker.

-inkle, crinkle, inkle, sprinkle, tinkle, twinkle, winkle, wrinkle; besprinkle; periwinkle.

-inkling, inkling, sprinkling, tinkling, twinkling, wrinkling.

-inky, blinky, dinky, inky, kinky, pinky; Helsinki.

-inland, Finland, inland.

-inly, inly, thinly; McKinley.

-inner, dinner, finner, grinner, inner, pinner, sinner, skinner, spinner, tinner, winner; beginner, muleskinner.

-innet, ginnet, linnet, minute, spinet.

-innier, finnier, linear, skinnier.

-innish. See **-inish.**

-innow, minnow, winnow.

-inny, finny, guinea, Guinea, hinny, mini, Minnie, ninny, pinny, Pliny, skinny, spinney, tinny, vinny, whinny, Winnie; ignominy.

-ino (-ī-), lino, rhino; albino.

-ino (-ē-). See **-eno.**

-inor. See **-iner.**

-inous. See **-inus.**

-inster, minster, Münster, spinster; Leominster, Westminster.

-intel, lintel, pintle, quintal.

-inter, dinter, hinter, minter, printer, splinter, sprinter, squinter, stinter, tinter, winter.

-into, pinto, Shinto.

-intry, splintery, vintry, wintry.

-inty, Dinty, flinty, glinty, linty, minty, squinty.

-inue, sinew; continue, retinue; discontinue.

-inus, dryness, highness, linous, Minos, minus, shyness, sinus, slyness, spinous, vinous; wryness, Aquinas, echinus, lupinus, salinous, Your Highness.

-inute. See **-innet.**

-iny (-ī-), briny, miny, piney, shiny, spiny, tiny, twiny, viny, whiney, winy; sunshiny.

-iny (-i-). See **-inny.**

-inyl. See **-inal.**

-io. See **-eo.**

-ion, Bryan, ion, lion, scion, Zion; anion, cation, O'Brien, Orion; dandelion.

-iot. See **-iet.**

-ious. See **-ias.**

-ipend, ripened, stipend.

-iper, diaper, griper, piper, riper, sniper, striper, swiper, typer, viper, wiper; bagpiper, sandpiper; windshield wiper.

-ipher. See **-ifer.**

-iple (-ī-), disciple, ectypal.

-iple (-i-). See **-ipple.**

-iplet, liplet, triplet.

-ipling. See **-ippling.**

-ippe. See **-ippy.**

-ipper, chipper, clipper, dipper, flipper, gypper, kipper, nipper, shipper, sipper, skipper, slipper, snipper, stripper, tipper, tripper, whipper; Yom Kippur.

-ippet, sippet, skippet, snippet, tippet, whippet.

-ippi. See **-ippy.**

-ipple, cripple, nipple, ripple, stipple, tipple, triple.

-ippling, crippling, Kipling, rippling, stippling, tippling.

-ippo, hippo, Lippo.

-ippy, chippy, drippy, grippy, lippy, nippy, slippy, snippy, zippy; Xanthippe; Mississippi.

-ipsy. See **-ypsy.**

-iptic. See **-yptic.**

-iquant. See **-ecant.**

-iquely. See **-eakly.**

-iquor. See **-icker.**

-ira, Ira, Myra; Elmira, hegira, Palmyra.

-irant, gyrant, spirant, tyrant; aspirant, conspirant, expirant.

-irate. See **-yrate.**

-irchen, birchen, urchin.

-irder. See **-urder.**

-irdie. See **-urdy.**

-irdle, curdle, girdle, hurdle; engirdle.

-irdly, birdly, curdly, thirdly; absurdly.

-ireling, hireling, squireling.

-irely, direly; entirely.

-ireme, bireme, trireme.

-iren, Byron, siren; environ.

-irgin. See **-urgeon.**

-irgy. See **-urgy.**

-iric. See **-yric.**

-iris. See **-irus.**

-irker, burker, irker, jerker, lurker, shirker, smirker, worker.

-irler. See **-urler.**

-irling. See **-urling.**

-irlish, churlish, girlish.

-irly. See **-urly.**

-irma. See **-urma.**

-irmant. See **-erment.**

-irmer, firmer, murmur, squirmer, termer; affirmer, confirmer, infirmer.

-irmish, firmish, skirmish, squirmish, wormish.

-irmy. See **-ermy.**

-iro, Cairo, giro, gyro, tyro; autogiro.

-iron. See **-iren.**

-irous. See **-irus.**

-irrup, chirrup, stirrup, syrup.

-irter. See **-erter.**

-irtle. See **-urtle.**

-irty, Bertie, cherty, dirty, flirty, Gertie, shirty, spurty, squirty, thirty.

-irus, Cyrus, irus, virus; desirous, Osiris, papyrus.

-iry, briery, diary, fiery, friary, miry, priory, spiry, squiry, wiry; enquiry.

-isal, reprisal; paradisal.

-iscal, discal, fiscal.

-iscount, discount, miscount.

-iscuit. See **-isket.**

-iscus, discus, discous, viscous; hibiscus, meniscus.

-isel. See **-izzle.**

-isely, nicely; concisely, precisely.

-iser. See **-isor.**

-isher, disher, fisher, fissure, swisher, wisher; kingfisher, well-wisher.

-ishy, fishy, swishy.

-isian. See **-ision.**

-isic. See **-ysic.**

-ision, vision; collision, concision, decision, derision, division, elision, Elysian, envision, excision, incision, misprision, Parisian, precision, prevision, provision, recision, rescission, revision; circumcision, Phonevision, stratovision, subdivision, supervision, television.

-isis, crisis, Isis, phthisis.

-isive, decisive, derisive, divisive, incisive; indecisive.

-isker, brisker, frisker, risker, whisker; bewhisker.

-isket, biscuit, brisket, tisket, trisket, wisket.

-isky, frisky, risky, whiskey.

-island, highland, island, Thailand.

-isly. See **-izzly.**

-ismal, dismal; abysmal, baptismal; cataclysmal, catechismal, paroxysmal.

-ison. See **-izen.**

-isor, Dreiser, geyser, Kaiser, miser, sizar, visor, wiser; adviser, divisor, incisor; appetizer, atomizer, energizer, fertilizer, supervisor.
   Also: **-ise** + **-er** (as in *reviser*, etc.)
   Also: **-ize** + **-er** (as in *sterilizer*, etc.)

-isper, crisper, lisper, whisper.

-ispy, crispy, lispy, wispy.

-issal. See **-istle.**

-issant. See **-ecent.**

-issile. See **-istle.**

-ission. See **-ition.**

-issor. See **-izzer.**

-issue, issue, tissue; reissue.

-issure. See **-isher.**

-istance, distance; assistance, consistence, existence, insistence, persistence, resistance, subsistence; coexistence, equidistance, nonexistence, nonresistance.

-istant, distant; assistant, consistent, existent, insistent, persistent, resistant, subsistent; coexistent, equidistant, inconsistent, nonexistent, nonresistant, preexistent.

-isten, christen, glisten, listen.

-istence. See **-istance.**

-istent. See **-istant.**

-ister, bister, blister, glister, mister, sister, twister; insister, persister, resister, transistor.

-istic, cystic, fistic, mystic; ballistic, deistic, juristic, linguistic, logistic, puristic, sadistic, simplistic, sophistic, statistic, stylistic, theistic, touristic; altruistic, anarchistic, animistic, atavistic, atheistic, bolshevistic, cabalistic, casuistic, catechistic, chauvinistic, communistic, egoistic, egotistic, euphemistic, fatalistic, humanistic, journalistic, nihilistic, optimistic, pantheistic, pessimistic, pietistic, pugilistic, realistic, socialistic, solecistic, syllogistic; anachronistic, capitalistic, characteristic, idealistic, polytheistic, rationalistic, ritualistic, sensualistic; materialistic, spiritualistic; individualistic.

-istin. See **-iston**

-istle, bristle, fissile, gristle, missal, missile, sissile, thistle, whistle; abyssal, dickcissel, dismissal, epistle.

-istmas, Christmas, isthmus.

-iston, Kristen, piston, Tristan; phlogiston, sacristan; amethystine.

-ita (-ē-), cheetah, pita, Rita, vita; Anita, Bomita, Granita, Juanita, Lolita, partita; incognita, Margarita, Margherita, señorita.

-itain. See **-itten.**

-ital, title, vital; entitle, recital, requital, subtitle.

-itan. See **-ighten.**

-itcher, ditcher, hitcher, itcher, pitcher, richer, stitcher, switcher.

-itchy, bitchy, hitchy, itchy, pitchy, twitchy.

-ite. See **-ighty.**

-iteful. See **-ightful.**

-itely. See **-ightly.**

-itement, excitement, incitement, indictment.

-iten. See **-ighten.**

-iter. See **-ighter.**

-itey. See **-ighty.**

-ither (-ī-), blither, either, lither, neither, tither, writher.

-ither (-i-), blither, dither, hither, thither, slither, whither, wither.

-ithing, scything, tithing, writhing.

-ithy, pithy, smithy.

-iti. See **-eaty.**

-itial. See **-icial.**

-itic, critic; arthritic, bronchitic, dendritic, Hamitic, Levitic, mephitic, proclitic, rachitic, Semitic; analytic, biolytic, catalytic, cenobitic, eremitic, hypocritic, Jesuitic, paralytic, parasitic; meteoritic; psychoanalytic.

-iting, biting, whiting; handwriting.

Also: **-ight** + **-ing** (as in *fighting*, etc.)
Also: **-ite** + **-ing** (as in *uniting*, etc.)
Also: **-ict** + **-ing** (as in *indicting*, etc.)

-ition, fission, mission; addition, admission, ambition, attrition, audition, cognition, coition, commission, condition, contrition, edition, emission, fruition, Galician, ignition, logician, magician, monition, munition, musician, nutrition, omission, optician, partition, patrician, perdition, permission, petition, physician, position, remission, rendition, sedition, submission, suspicion, tactician, tradition, transition, transmission, tuition, volition; abolition, acquisition, admonition, ammunition, apparition, apposition, coalition, competition, composition, definition, demolition, deposition, disposition, disquisition, ebullition, electrician, erudition, exhibition, expedition, exposition, extradition, imposition, inanition, inhibition, intermission, intuition, manumission, obstetrician, opposition, parturition, politician, premonition, preposition, prohibition, proposition, recognition, repetition, requisition, rhetorician, statistician, superstition, supposition, transposition; academician, arithmetician, decomposition, dialectician, geometrician, indisposition, inquisition; interposition, juxtaposition, mathematician, metaphysician, predisposition, presupposition.

-itious. See **-icious.**

-itle. See **-ital.**

-itness, fitness, witness.

-iton (-ī-). See **-ighten.**

-iton (-i-). See **-itten.**

-itsy. See **-itzy.**

-ittal. See **-ittle.**

-ittance, pittance, quittance; acquittance, admittance, remittance, transmittance; intermittance.

-ittee. See **-itty.**

-itten, bitten, Britain, Briton, kitten, Lytton, mitten, smitten, written; hard-bitten.

-itter, bitter, fitter, flitter, fritter, fritter, glitter, hitter, jitter, knitter, litter, pitter, quitter, sitter, spitter, splitter, titter, twitter; atwitter, committer, embitter, transmitter; babysitter, counterfeiter.

-itti. See **-itty.**

-ittle, brittle, knittle, little, skittle, spittle, tittle, victual, whittle; acquittal, belittle, committal, lickspittle, remittal, transmittal.

-ittler, victualler, whittler; belittler.

-itty, city, ditty, flitty, gritty, kitty, Kitty, nitty, pity, pretty, witty; banditti, committee; nitty-gritty, Salt Lake City, subcommittee, Walter Mitty.

-itual, ritual; habitual.

-ity. See **-itty.**

-itzy, Fritzy, Mitzi, Ritzy; itsy bitsy.

-ival, rival; archival, arrival, revival, survival; adjectival, conjunctival; imperatival, nominatival.

-ivance, connivance, contrivance, survivance.

-ivel, civil, drivel, shrivel, snivel, swivel; uncivil.

-iven, driven, given, riven, scriven, shriven; forgiven.

-iver (-iv-), flivver, giver, liver, quiver, river, shiver, sliver; deliver, forgiver.

-iver (-ī-), diver, driver, fiver, hiver, Ivor, shriver, skiver; conniver, contriver, deriver, reviver, survivor.

-ivet, civet, pivot, divot, privet, rivet, trivet.

-ivid, livid, vivid.

-ivil. See **-ivel.**

-ivor. See **-iver.**

-ivot. See **-ivet.**

-ivver. See **-iver.**

-ivvy. See **-ivy.**

-ivy, civvy, divvy, Livy, privy, skivvy, tivy; tantivy.

-ixer, fixer, mixer; elixir.

-ixie, Dixie, nixie, pixie, tricksy.

-ixture, fixture, mixture; admixture, commixture, immixture; intermixture.

-izard. See **-izzard.**

-izen (-ī-), dizen; bedizen, horizon.

-izen (-i-), dizen, mizzen, prison, wizen; arisen, bedizen, imprison.

-izier. See **-izzier.**

-izzard, blizzard, gizzard, izzard, lizard, scissored, vizard, wizard.

-izzer, quizzer, scissor, whizzer.

-izzier, busier, dizzier, frizzier, vizier.

-izzle, chisel, drizzle, fizzle, frizzle, grizzle, mizzle, sizzle, swizzle.

-izzly, drizzly, frizzly, grisly, grizzly, sizzly.

-izzy, busy, dizzy, frizzy, Lizzie, tizzy.

-oa, boa, Goa, moa, Noah, proa; aloha, Genoa, jerboa, Samoa; Krakatoa, protozoa, Shenandoah.

-oader, goader, loader, Oder, odor; breech-loader, corroder, exploder, foreboder, free-loader, malodor; muzzleloader.

-oaken. See **-oken.**

-oaker. See **-oker.**

-oaky. See **-oky.**

-oaler. See **-oller.**

-oaly. See **-oly.**

-oamer. See **-omer.**

-oaner. See **-oner.**

-oarder. See **-order.**

-oarer. See **-orer.**

-oarish, boarish, whorish.

-oarsely, coarsely, hoarsely.

-oary. See **-ory.**

-oastal, coastal, postal.

-oaster, boaster, coaster, poster, roaster, toaster; bill-poster, four-poster; roller coaster.

-oaten, croton, oaten; verboten.

-oater. See **-otor.**

-oatswain. See **-osen.**

-oaty, dhoti, floaty, goatee, oaty, throaty, zloty; chayote, coyote, peyote; Don Quixote.

-obate, globate, probate.

-obber, blobber, clobber, cobber, jobber, lobber, robber, slobber, sobber, swabber, throbber.

-obbin, bobbin, Dobbin, robbin, robin, Robin.

-obble, cobble, gobble, hobble, nobble, squabble, wobble.

-obbler, cobbler, gobbler, squabbler, wobbler.

-obby, bobby, Bobby, cobby, hobby, knobby, lobby, mobby, Robbie, snobby.

-obe, obi, Gobi, Toby; adobe, Nairobi.

-ober, prober, sober; disrober, October.

-obin. See **-obbin.**

-obo, hobo, lobo, oboe.

-obster, lobster, mobster.

-ocal, focal, local, vocal, yokel; bifocal.

-occer. See **-ocker.**

-ocean. See **-otion.**

-ocer, closer, grocer, grosser; engrosser, jocoser, moroser.

-ochee. See **-oky.**

-ocher. See **-oker.**

-ocile. See **-ostle.**

-ocious, atrocious, ferocious, precocious.

-ocker, blocker, clocker, cocker, docker, Fokker, knocker, locker, mocker, rocker, shocker, soccer, socker, stocker; beta blocker, knickerbocker.

-ocket, brocket, Crockett, docket, locket, pocket, rocket, socket, sprocket; pickpocket, skyrocket, vest-pocket.

-ockey. See **-ocky.**

-ocky, cocky, crocky, flocky, hockey, jockey, locky, rocky, sake, Saki, schlocky, stocky; Iraqi; jabberwocky, Kawasaki, Nagasaki, sukiyaki, teriyaki.

-oco, coco, cocoa, loco; baroco, rococo; locofoco, Orinoco; poco a poco.

-ocoa. See **-oco.**

-ocre. See **-oker.**

-octer. See **-octor.**

-oction, concoction, decoction.

-octor, doctor, proctor; concocter, decocter.

-ocus, crocus, focus, hocus, locus; Hohokus; hocus-pocus.

-ocust, focused, locust.

-oda, coda, Rhoda, soda; Baroda, pagoda.

-odal, modal, nodal, yodel.

-odden, sodden, trodden; downtrodden, untrodden.

-odder, dodder, fodder, nodder, odder, plodder, prodder, solder.

-oddess, bodice, goddess.

-odding, codding, nodding, plodding, podding, prodding, wadding.

-oddle, coddle, model, noddle, swaddle, toddle, twaddle, waddle; remodel; mollycoddle.

-oddy. See **-ody.**

-odel (-o-). See **-oddle.**

-odel (-ō-). See **-odal.**

-oder. See **-oader.**

-odest, bodiced, modest, oddest; immodest.

-odger, codger, dodger, Dodger, lodger, Roger.

-odic, anodic, iodic, melodic, methodic, rhapsodic, spasmodic, synodic; episodic, periodic.

-odice. See **-oddess.**

-odling, coddling, codling, godling, modeling, swaddling, toddling, twaddling, waddling.

-odly, godly, oddly; ungodly.

-odo, dodo; Quasimodo.

-odor. See **-oader.**

-odule, module, nodule.

-ody, body, cloddy, Mahdi, noddy, Roddy, shoddy, soddy, toddy, wadi; embody, nobody, somebody; anybody, busybody, everybody.

-oeia. See **-ea.**

-oem, poem, proem; jeroboam.

-oeman. See **-omen.**

-oer. See **-ower.**

-offal, offal, waffle.

-offee, coffee, toffee.

-offer, coffer, cougher, doffer, goffer, offer, proffer, scoffer.

-offin. See **-often.**

-offing, coughing, doffing, offing, scoffing.

-often, coffin, dauphin, often, soften.

-ofty, lofty, softy.

-oga, toga, yoga; Saratoga; Ticonderoga.

-ogan, brogan, hogan, Hogan, shogun, slogan.

-oger. See **-odger.**

-ogey. See **-ogie.**

-oggish, doggish, froggish, hoggish

-oggle, boggle, coggle, goggle, joggle, toggle; boondoggle, hornswoggle.

-oggy, boggy, cloggy, doggy, foggy, froggy, groggy, joggy, soggy.

-ogi. See **-ogie.**

-ogie, bogey, bogie, dogie, fogey, stogie, Yogi.

-ogle, bogle, Gogol, ogle.

-oic, stoic; azoic, benzoic, heroic; Cenozoic,

Eozoic, Mesozoic, unheroic, protozoic; Paleozoic.

-oidal, colloidal, spheroidal; asteroidal, ellipsoidal, trapezoidal.

-oider, voider; avoider, embroider.

-oily, coyly, doily, oily, roily.

-oiner, coiner; enjoiner, purloiner.

-ointer, jointer, pointer; anointer.

-ointment, ointment; anointment, appointment, disjointment; disappointment.

-oister, cloister, foister, hoister, moister, oyster, roister.

-oiter, goiter, loiter; exploiter, reconnoiter.

-okay, croquet, okay, Tokay.

-okel. See **-ocal.**

-oken, broken, oaken, spoken, token, woken; bespoken, betoken, foretoken, heartbroken, housebroken, Hoboken, outspoken, plainspoken, unbroken, unspoken.

-oker, broker, choker, cloaker, croaker, joker, ocher, poker, soaker, smoker, stoker, stroker, yoker, convoker, evoker, invoker, provoker, revoker, stockbroker; mediocre.

-okey. See **-oky.**

-okum, hokum, locum, oakum.

-oky, choky, croaky, hokey, jokey, oaky, poky, soaky, smoky, troche, trochee; hokypoky, karaoke, okey-dokey.

-ola, cola, kola, Lola, Nola, Zola; Angola, canola, gondola, granola, payola, viola; ayatollah, Española, gladiola, Gorgonzola, Hispaniola, Pensacola, roseola.

-olar (-o-). See **-ollar.**

-olar (-ō-). See **-oller.**

-olden, golden, olden; beholden, embolden.

-older (-ōl-), bolder, boulder, colder, folder, holder, molder, moulder, older, shoulder, smolder; beholder, householder, upholder.

-older (-od-). See **-odder.**

-oleful, bowlful, doleful, soulful.

-olely. See **-oly.**

-olemn. See **-olumn.**

-olen. See **-olon.**

-oler (-o-). See **-ollar.**

-oler (-ō-). See **-oller.**

-olic, colic, frolic, rollick; bucolic, carbolic, embolic, symbolic, systolic; alcoholic, apostolic, diastolic, diabolic, epistolic, hyperbolic, melancholic, metabolic, parabolic, vitriolic.

-olid, solid, squalid, stolid.

-olish, polish; abolish, demolish.

-ollar, choler, collar, dollar, loller, scholar, squalor.

-ollard, bollard, Lollard, pollard.

-ollege. See **-owledge.**

-ollen. See **-olon.**

-oller, bowler, coaler, doler, droller, molar, polar, poller, roller, solar, stroller, toller, troller; cajoler, comptroller, consoler, controller, enroller, extoller, patroller, bankroller, steamroller.

-ollick. See **-olic.**

-ollie. See **-olly.**

-ollins, Collins, Hollins, Rollins.

-ollo. See **-ollow.**

-ollop, dollop, lollop, scallop, trollop, Trollope, wallop.

-ollow, follow, hollow, Rollo, swallow, wallow; Apollo.

-olly (-o-), Bali, collie, Dollie, dolly, folly, golly, holly, jolly, Molly, polly, Polly, trolley, volley; finale, loblolly, tamale; melancholy.

-olly (-ō-). See **-oly.**

-olo, bolo, polo, solo; Marco Polo.

-olon, colon, solon, Solon, stolen, swollen; semicolon.

-olonel. See **-ernal.**

-olor. See **-uller.**

-olster, bolster, holster; upholster.

-olter, bolter, colter, jolter, poulter; revolter.

-oltish, coltish, doltish.

-olumn, column, solemn.

-olver, solver; absolver, dissolver, evolver, resolver, revolver.

-oly (-ō-), drolly, goalie, holy, lowly, moly, shoaly, slowly, solely, wholly; aioli, cannoli, frijole, Stromboli; guacamole, ravioli, roly-poly.

-oly (-o-). See **-olly.**

-oma, coma, Roma, soma; aboma, aroma, diploma, Natoma, sarcoma, Tacoma; carcinoma, la paloma, Oklahoma.

-omach, hummock, stomach.

-omain, domain, ptomaine, romaine.

-oman. See **-omen.**

-ombat, combat, wombat.

-omber. See **-omer.**

-ombie, Dombey, zombie; Abercrombie.

-omely. See **-umbly.**

-omen, bowman, foeman, gnomon, omen,

Roman, showman, yeoman; abdomen, cognomen.

-oment, foment, moment; bestowment.

-omer (-ō-), comber, homer, Homer, omer, roamer; beachcomber, misnomer.

-omer (-u-). See **-ummer.**

-omet, comet, grommet, vomit.

-omic, comic, gnomic; atomic; agronomic, anatomic, astronomic, autonomic, diatomic, economic, monatomic, taxonomic.

-omit. See **-omet.**

-omma. See **-ama.**

-ommy. See **-almy.**

-omo, chromo, Como, homo, promo; majordomo.

-ompass, compass, rumpus; encompass.

-onal, clonal, tonal, zonal; atonal, hormonal.

-onday. See **-undy.**

-ondent, fondant, frondent; despondent, respondent; co-respondent, correspondent.

-onder, blonder, bonder, condor, fonder, ponder, squander, wander, yonder; absconder, desponder, responder; corresponder.

-one. See **-ony.**

-onely. See **-only.**

-onent, sonant; component, deponent, exponent, opponent, proponent.

-oner, boner, donor, droner, groaner, loaner, loner, moaner, owner, phoner; atoner, condoner, intoner, landowner.

-onest, honest, non est, wannest; dishonest.

-oney (-ō-). See **-ony.**

-oney (-u-). See **-unny.**

-onger (-o-), conger, longer, stronger.

-onger (-u-). See **-unger.**

-onging, longing, thronging, wronging; belonging, prolonging.

-ongly, strongly, wrongly.

-ongo, bongo, Congo, Mongo.

-oni. See **-ony.**

-onic, chronic, chthonic, conic, phonic, sonic, tonic; Aaronic, agonic, bubonic, Byronic, canonic, carbonic, colonic, cyclonic, demonic, draconic, euphonic, harmonic, hedonic, ionic, ironic, laconic, masonic, mnemonic, platonic, sardonic, Slavonic, symphonic, tectonic, Teutonic; diaphonic, diatonic, electronic, embryonic, histrionic, Housatonic, hydroponic, isotonic, macaronic, monophonic, philharmonic, polyphonic, Solomonic, telephonic, ultrasonic; architectonic, stereophonic.

-onion, bunion, Bunyan, onion, Runyon, trunion.

-onish, donnish, wannish; admonish, astonish, premonish.

-onkey. See **-unky.**

-only, lonely, only.

-onnet, bonnet, sonnet.

-onnie, Bonnie, bonny, Connie, Johnny, Lonny, Ronnie.

-onor (-o-), goner, honor, wanner; dishonor, marathoner.

-onor (-ō-). See **-oner.**

-onsil, consul, tonsil; proconsul, responsal.

-onsul. See **-onsil.**

-ontal. See **-untle.**

-onter. See **-unter.**

-ontract, contract, entr'acte.

-onus, bonus, Cronus, Jonas, onus, slowness; colonus.

-ony, bony, Coney, cony, crony, drony, phony, pony, stony, Toni, tony, Tony; baloney, Marconi, Shoshone, spumoni, tortoni; abalone, alimony, antimony, cannelloni, ceremony, cicerone, macaroni, matrimony, minestrone, palimony, rigatoni, parsimony, patrimony, sanctimony, testimony, zabaglione.

-ooby, booby, ruby, Ruby.

-oocher. See **-uture.**

-ooding, hooding, pudding.

-oodle, boodle, doodle, feudal, noodle, strudel; caboodle, flapdoodle; Yankee Doodle.

-oody (-ŏŏ-), goody, woody.

-oody (-ōō-), broody, Judy, moody, Trudy.

-oody (-u-). See **-uddy.**

-ooey. See **-ewy.**

-ookie. See **-ooky.**

-ookish, bookish, rookish, spookish.

-ooky (-ŏŏ-), bookie, cooky, hookey, hooky, rookie.

-ooky (-ōō-), fluky, kooky, spooky; Kabuki.

-oolie. See **-uly.**

-oolish, coolish, foolish, mulish.

-oolly (-ŏŏ-). See **-ully.**

-oolly (-ōō-). See **-uly.**

-oomer. See **-umer.**

-oomy, bloomy, gloomy, plumy, rheumy, roomy.

-ooner. See **-uner.**

-oony, loony, moony, spoony.

-ooper, blooper, cooper, grouper, hooper, snooper, stupor, super, trooper, whooper; pooper-scooper; superduper.

-oopy, croupy, droopy, rupee, soupy, whoopee.

-oorish, boorish, Moorish.

-ooser. See **-oser.**

-oosy (-ōō zi). See **-oozy.**

-oosy (-ōō si). See **-uicy.**

-ooter, cuter, hooter, looter, mooter, neuter, pewter, rooter, scooter, tutor; commuter, computer, disputer, freebooter, polluter, recruiter, refuter; coadjutor, prosecutor.

-oothless. See **-uthless.**

-ootie. See **-ooty.**

-ooty, beauty, booty, cootie, cutie, duty, fluty, fruity, rooty, snooty, sooty; agouti, Djibouti; tutti-frutti.

-ooza. See **-usa.**

-oozer. See **-oser.**

-oozle, foozle, fusel, ousel; bamboozle, perusal, refusal.

-oozy, boozy, floosie, newsy, oozy, woosy.

-opal, opal, copal; Adrianople, Constantinople.

-oper (-ō-), groper, moper, roper, sloper, toper; eloper, interloper.

-oper (-o-). See **-opper.**

-opey. See **-opy.**

-ophy. Sophie, strophe, trophy.

-opic, topic, tropic; myopic; microscopic, misanthropic, philanthropic, presbyopic, spectroscopic, telescopic; heliotropic, kaleidoscopic, stereoscopic.

-ople. See **-opal.**

-opper, chopper, copper, cropper, hopper, popper, proper, shopper, stopper, topper, whopper; clodhopper, cornpopper, eavesdropper, grasshopper, improper, namedropper, sharecropper, show-stopper; window-shopper.

-opping, chopping, sopping, topping, whopping; eye-popping, name-dropping; window-shopping.

    Also: **-opp** + **-ing** (as in *shopping*, etc.)

-opple, stoppel, topple; estoppel.

-oppy, choppy, copy, floppy, Hoppy, poppy, sloppy, soppy; jalopy; photocopy.

-opsy, dropsy, Topsy; autopsy, biopsy.

-opter, copter; adopter; helicopter.

-optic, coptic, optic; synoptic.

-option, option; adoption.

-opy (-ō-), dopey, Hopi, mopy, ropy, soapy, topee.

-opy (-o-). See **-oppy.**

-ora, aura, Cora, Dora, flora, Flora, hora, Laura, mora, Nora, Torah; Andorra, angora, Aurora, fedora, Marmora, menorah, Pandora, signora; Floradora, Leonora.

-orage, borage, porridge, shorage, storage.

-oral, aural, chloral, choral, coral, floral, horal, laurel, moral, oral, quarrel, sorrel; auroral, immoral, sororal.

-orax, borax, storax, thorax.

-orbel. See **-arble.**

-orchard, orchard, tortured.

-orcher, scorcher, torture.

-order, boarder, border, forder, hoarder, order, warder; disorder, recorder, rewarder.

-ordon, cordon, Gordon, Jordan, warden.

-ordy. See **-urdy.**

-ore. See **-ory.**

-orehead. See **-orrid.**

-oreign, florin, foreign, warren.

-orer, borer, corer, horror, roarer, scorer, snorer; abhorrer, adorer, explorer, ignorer, restorer.

-oresail. See **-orsel.**

-orest, florist, forest, sorest.

-orey. See **-ory.**

-organ, gorgon, Morgan, organ.

-orger, forger, gorger, ordure; disgorger.

-ori. See **-ory.**

-oric, chloric, choric, Doric, Yorick; caloric, euphoric, historic, phosphoric; allegoric, metaphoric, meteoric, paregoric, prehistoric, sophomoric; phantasmagoric.

-orid. See **-orrid.**

-oris, Boris, Doris, loris, Horace, Morris, Norris.

-orker. See **-irker.**

-ormal, formal, normal; abnormal, informal, subnormal; paranormal.

-orman, doorman, floorman, foreman, Mormon, Norman; longshoreman; Anglo-Norman.

-ormant, dormant; conformant, informant.

-ormer, dormer, former, stormer, warmer; barnstormer, conformer, informer, performer, reformer, transformer.

-ormish. See **-irmish.**

-ormy. See **-ermy.**

-orner, corner, horner, mourner, scorner, warner; adorner, suborner.

-ornet, cornet, hornet.

-orney. See **-ourney.**

-ornful, mournful, scornful.

-orning, morning, mourning, scorning, warning; adorning, forewarning.

-orny, corny, horny, thorny.

-orough, borough, burro, burrow, furrow, thorough.

-orous, chorus, porous, Taurus, torous, torus; decorous, imporous, pylorus, sonorous; brontosaurus, stegosaurus, ichthyosaurus.

-orpor, torpor, warper.

-orpus, corpus, porpoise.

-orrel. See **-oral.**

-orrent, torrent, warrant; abhorrent.

-orrid, florid, forehead, horrid, torrid.

-orridge. See **-orage.**

-orris. See **-oris.**

-orror. See **-orer.**

-orrow, borrow, morrow, sorrow; tomorrow.

-orry (-o-), quarry, sorry. See also **-arry** and **-ory.**

-orry (-û-). See **-urry.**

-orsel, dorsal, foresail, morsel.

-orsen. See **-erson.**

-orsion. See **-ortion.**

-ortal, chortle, mortal, portal; immortal.

-orten, Horton, Morton, Norton, quartan, shorten.

-orter, mortar, porter, quarter, shorter, snorter, sorter; contorter, distorter, ex-

porter, extorter, importer, reporter, rip-
snorter, supporter.

-ortex, cortex, vortex.

-ortion, portion, torsion; abortion, apportion,
consortion, contortion, distortion, extor-
tion, proportion; disproportion.

-ortive, sportive, tortive; abortive, transport-
ive.

-ortle. See **-ortal.**

-ortly, courtly, portly.

-ortment, assortment, comportment, deport-
ment, disportment, transportment.

-orton. See **-orten.**

-ortune, fortune; importune, misfortune.

-orture. See **-orcher.**

-ortured. See **-orchard.**

-orty, forty, snorty, sortie, warty; pianoforte.

-orum, forum, quorum; decorum; ad va-
lorem, indecorum, variorum; sanctum
sanctorum, schola cantorum.

-orus. See **-orous.**

-ory, dory, flory, glory, gory, hoary, lorry,
storey, story, Tory; Old Glory, vainglory;
allegory, a priori, category, con amore,
desultory, dilatory, dormitory, gustatory,
hortatory, hunky dory, inventory, lauda-
tory, mandatory, migratory, offertory, ora-
tory, peremptory, predatory, prefatory,
promissory, promontory, purgatory, reper-
tory, territory; a fortiori, cacciatore, circu-
latory, commendatory, compensatory, con-
ciliatory, conservatory, declaratory,
defamatory, depilatory, depository, depre-
catory, derogatory, exclamatory, explana-
tory, inflammatory, laboratory, obligatory,

observatory, preparatory, reformatory, respiratory, undulatory; a posteriori, retaliatory. See also **-orry.**

-osa, osa; Formosa, mimosa; Mariposa, virtuosa.

-osely, closely, grossly, jocosely, morosely, verbosely.

-osen, chosen, frozen, boatswain, hosen.

-oser (-o͞o zər), boozer, bruiser, chooser, cruiser, loser. See also **-user.**

-oser (-o sər). See **-ocer.**

-oset. See **-osit.**

-osher, josher, washer.

-oshy, boshy, sloshy, squashy, swashy, washy.

-osier, crosier, hosier, osier.

-osion, ambrosian, corrosion, erosion, explosion, implosion.

-osit, closet, posit; deposit.

-osive, corrosive, erosive, explosive, implosive.

-oso. See **-uso.**

-ossal. See **-ostle.**

-osser. See **-ocer.**

-ossil. See **-ostle.**

-ossom, blossom, possum; opossum.

-ossum. See **-ossom.**

-ossy, bossy, drossy, Flossie, flossy, glossy, mossy, posse, quasi, tossy.

-ostal, costal, hostel, hostile; infracostal, intercostal, Pentecostal.

-oster (-o-), coster, foster, Gloucester, roster; accoster, imposter; paternoster, Pentecoster.

-oster (-ō-). See **-oaster.**

-ostic, caustic, gnostic; acrostic, agnostic, prognostic; anacrostic, diagnostic, paracrostic, pentacostic.

-ostle, docile, dossil, fossil, jostle, throstle, wassail; apostle, colossal.

-ostler, hostler, jostler, ostler, wassailer.

-ostly, ghostly, mostly.

-ostril, costrel, nostril, rostral.

-ostrum, nostrum, rostrum.

-osure, closure; composure, disclosure, enclosure, exposure, foreclosure, reposure; discomposure.

-osy, cosy, dozy, nosy, posy, prosy, Rosie, rosy.

-ota, quota, rota; Dakota, iota; Minnesota.

-otal, dotal, notal, rotal, total; sclerotal, teetotal; anecdotal, antidotal, extradotal, sacerdotal.

-otcher, blotcher, botcher, notcher, splotcher, watcher; topnotcher.

-otchy, blotchy, boccie, botchy, splotchy; huarache, vivace; Liberace, Pagliacci.

-ote. See **-oaty.**

-otem, totem; factotum.

-oter. See **-otor.**

-other (-o-), bother, father, fother, pother.

-other (-u-), brother, mother, other, smother; another.

-othing, clothing, loathing.

-othy, frothy, mothy.

-otic, chaotic, demotic, despotic, erotic, exotic, hypnotic, narcotic, neurotic, osmotic, pyrotic, quixotic, zymotic; idiotic, patriotic; macrobiotic.

-otion, Goshen, lotion, motion, notion, ocean, potion; commotion, devotion, emotion, promotion, remotion; locomotion.

-otive, motive, votive; emotive, promotive; locomotive.

-otly, hotly, motley, squatly.

-oto, Oto, photo, toto; De Soto, Kyoto.

-otor, boater, bloater, doter, floater, motor, quoter, rotor, voter; promoter; locomotor.

-ottage, cottage, pottage, wattage.

-ottar. See **-otter.**

-otten, cotton, gotten, Groton, rotten; begotten, forgotten; misbegotten.

-otter, blotter, clotter, cottar, cotter, dotter, hotter, jotter, knotter, ottar, otter, plotter, potter, rotter, squatter, spotter, swatter, totter, trotter; complotter.

-ottish, schottische, Scottish, sottish.

-ottle, bottle, dottle, glottal, mottle, pottle, throttle, tottle, twattle, wattle; bluebottle; Aristotle.

-otto, blotto, grotto, lotto, motto, Otto, Watteau. See also **-ato** (-ä-).

-otton. See **-otten.**

-otty, blotty, clotty, dotty, knotty, Lottie, potty, snotty, spotty.

-ouble, bubble, double, rubble, stubble, trouble; body double.

-oubly. See **-ubbly.**

-oubter. See **-outer.**

-oucher, croucher, Goucher, sloucher, voucher.

-ouder. See **-owder.**

-oudy. See **-owdy.**

-oughen, roughen, toughen.

-ougher (-o-). See **-offer.**

-ougher (-u-). See **-uffer.**

-oughly. See **-uffly.**

-oughty. See **-outy.**

-oulder. See **-older.**

-oulful. See **-oleful.**

-ouncil, council, counsel, groundsel.

-ounder, bounder, flounder, founder, hounder, pounder, rounder, sounder; confounder, expounder, propounder.

-oundly, roundly, soundly; profoundly, unsoundly.

-ounger. See **-unger.**

-ountain, fountain, mountain.

-ounter, counter, mounter; accounter, discounter, encounter, surmounter.

-ounty, bounty, county, mounty.

-ouper. See **-ooper.**

-ouple, couple, supple.

-oupy. See **-oopy.**

-ourage, courage; demurrage, discourage, encourage.

-ouri. See **-ury.**

-ourish, currish, flourish, nourish.

-ourist. See **-urist.**

-ourly, hourly, sourly.

-ourney, Bernie, Ernie, gurney, journey, tourney; attorney.

-ournful. See **-ornful.**

-ourning. See **-orning.**

-ousal, housel, ousel, spousal, tousle; arousal, carousal, espousal.

-ousel. See **-ousal.**

-ouser, browser, dowser, houser, Mauser, mouser, rouser, schnauzer, towser, trouser; carouser.

-ousin. See **-ozen.**

-ousle. See **-ousal.**

-ousseau. See **-uso.**

-ousy, blowsy, drowsy, frowsy, lousy, mousy.

-outer, clouter, doubter, flouter, pouter, router, scouter, shouter, stouter, touter.

-outhful. See **-uthful.**

-outy, doughty, droughty, gouty, grouty, pouty, snouty.

-ova, nova, ova; Jehovah; Casanova, supernova, Villanova.

-oval, approval, disproval, removal, reproval; disapproval.

-ovel, grovel, hovel, novel.

-ovement, movement; approvement, improvement.

-oven (-ō-), cloven, coven, woven; Beethoven, handwoven; interwoven.

-oven (-u-), coven, oven, sloven.

-over (-ō-), clover, Dover, drover, over, plover, rover, stover, trover; crossover, flyover, hangover, Hanover, leftover, moreover, Passover, pullover, pushover, stopover.

-over (-u-), cover, lover, plover, shover; discover, recover, uncover.

-oward, coward, cowered, flowered, Howard, powered, showered, towered; highpowered; ivory-towered.

-owboy, cowboy, ploughboy.

-owder, chowder, crowder, louder, powder, prouder.

-owdy, cloudy, dowdy, howdy, rowdy; pandowdy.

-owel, bowel, dowel, rowel, towel, trowel, vowel; avowal; disembowel.

-ower (-ou-), bower, cower, dower, flour, flower, glower, hour, lower, our, power, scour, shower, sour, tower; cornflower, deflower, devour, empower, mayflower, safflower, sunflower, wallflower, watchtower, wildflower, willpower; cauliflower, overpower, passionflower, Schopenhauer, superpower, sweet-and-sour, thundershower, waterpower.

-ower (-ō-), blower, crower, goer, grower, knower, lower, mower, ower, rower, sewer, slower, sower, thrower, tower; bestower; overthrower.

-owered. See **-oward.**

-owery, bowery, cowry, dowry, flowery, houri, Maori, showery, towery.

-owing, blowing, crowing, flowing, glowing, going, growing, knowing, lowing, mowing, owing, rowing, sewing, showing, snowing, sowing, stowing, towing, throwing; mindblowing, seagoing.

    Also: **-ow** + **-ing** (as in *bestowing,* etc.)

    Also: **-o** + **-ing** (as in *outgoing,* etc.)

-owledge, college, knowledge; acknowledge, foreknowledge.

-owler. See **-oller.**

-owly. See **-oly.**

-owman. See **-omen.**

-owner. See **-oner.**

-ownie. See **-owny.**

-owny, brownie, Brownie, downy, frowny, towny.

-owry. See **-owery.**

-owsy. See **-ousy.**

-owy, blowy, Bowie, Chloë, doughy, glowy, Joey, showy, snowy, Zoë.

-oxen, coxswain, oxen.

-oxy, Coxey, doxy, foxy, moxie, proxy; Biloxi; orthodoxy, paradoxy; heterodoxy.

-oyal, loyal, royal; disloyal.

-oyalty, loyalty, royalty.

-oyance buoyance; annoyance, clairvoyance, flamboyance.

-oyant, buoyant, clairvoyant, flamboyant.

-oyer, annoyer, destroyer, employer, enjoyer.

-oyly. See **-oily.**

-oyment, deployment, employment, enjoyment; unemployment.

-oyster. See **-oister.**

-ozen (-u-), cousin, cozen, dozen.

-ozen (-ō-). See **-osen.**

-ozzle, nozzle, schnozzle.

-uager. See **-ager.**

-ual. See **-uel.**

-uant, fluent, truant; pursuant.

-uba, Cuba, juba, scuba, tuba; Aruba.

-ubbard. See **-upboard.**

-ubber, blubber, clubber, drubber, dubber, grubber, lubber, rubber, scrubber, snubber, stubber; landlubber; money-grubber; india rubber.

-ubberd. See **-upboard.**

-ubbish, clubbish, cubbish, grubbish, rubbish, tubbish.

-ubble. See **-ouble.**

-ubbly, bubbly, doubly, knubbly, rubbly, stubbly.

-ubby, chubby, cubby, grubby, hubby, nubby, scrubby, shrubby, stubby, tubby.

-ubic, cubic, pubic; cherubic.

-ubtle. See **-uttle.**

-ubtler. See **-utler.**

-uby. See **-ooby.**

-ucent, lucent; abducent, adducent, traducent, translucent.

-ucid, deuced, lucid, mucid; pellucid.

-ucker, bucker, chukker, ducker, mucker, pucker, succor, sucker, trucker, tucker; sapsucker, seersucker.

-uckett, bucket, tucket; Nantucket, Pawtucket.

-uckle, buckle, chuckle, huckle, knuckle, muckle, suckle, truckle; Arbuckle, bareknuckle, pinochle, swashbuckle, unbuckle; honeysuckle.

-uckled. See **-uckold.**

-uckler, buckler, chuckler, knuckler; swashbuckler.

-uckling, buckling, duckling, suckling.

-uckold, cuckold.
    Also: **-uckle** + **-d** (as in *buckled*, etc.)

-ucky, ducky, lucky, mucky, plucky; Kentucky, unlucky.

-ucre. See **-uker.**

-ucter. See **-uctor.**

-uction, fluxion, ruction, suction; abduction,

adduction, affluxion, conduction, construction, deduction, defluxion, destruction, effluxion, induction, influxion, instruction, production, reduction, seduction, traduction; deconstruction, introduction, misconstruction, reconstruction, reproduction; overproduction, superinduction.

-uctive, adductive, conductive, constructive, deductive, destructive, inductive, instructive, obstructive, productive, reductive, seductive, traductive; introductive, reproductive, superstructive; overproductive.

-uctor, ductor; abductor, adductor, conductor, constructor, destructor, eductor, instructor, obstructer; nonconductor.

-udder, dudder, flooder, mudder, rudder, scudder, shudder, udder.

-uddhist. See **-udist.**

-uddle, cuddle, huddle, muddle, puddle, ruddle.

-uddler, cuddler, huddler, muddler.

-uddy, bloody, buddy, cruddy, muddy, ruddy, studdy, study; fuddy-duddy, understudy.

-udel. See **-oodle.**

-udely, crudely, lewdly, nudely, rudely, shrewdly.

-udent, prudent, student; concludent, imprudent; jurisprudent.

-udest. See **-udist.**

-udgeon, bludgeon, dudgeon, gudgeon; curmudgeon.

-udgy, pudgy, smudgy.

-udish, crudish, dudish, lewdish, nudish, prudish, rudish, shrewdish.

-udist, Buddhist, crudest, feudist, lewdest, nudist, rudest, shrewdest.

-udo, judo, kudo, pseudo; escudo, testudo.

-udy. See **-uddy.**

-uel, crewel, cruel, dual, duel, fuel, gruel, jewel, newel; accrual, bejewel, eschewal, pursual, refuel, renewal, reviewal, subdual.

-uet, bluet, cruet, suet, intuit.

-uey. See **-ewy.**

-uffel. See **-uffle.**

-uffer, bluffer, buffer, duffer, gruffer, huffer, puffer, rougher, snuffer, stuffer, suffer, tougher.

-uffin, muffin, puffin; ragamuffin.

-uffing, bluffing, cuffing, huffing, puffing, stuffing.

-uffle, buffle, duffel, muffle, ruffle, scuffle, shuffle, snuffle, truffle.

-uffly, bluffly, gruffly, roughly, ruffly, shuf-fly, snuffly, toughly.

-uffy, fluffy, huffy, puffy, snuffy, scruffy, stuffy.

-ufty, mufti, tufty.

-ugal. See **-ugle.**

-ugger, bugger, drugger, hugger, lugger, plugger, rugger, smugger, snugger, tugger; hugger-mugger.

-uggle, juggle, smuggle, snuggle, struggle.

-uggy, buggy, muggy, puggy, sluggy.

-ugle, Breughel, bugle, frugal, fugal, kugel; MacDougall.

-ugly, smugly, snuggly, snugly, ugly.

-uicy, goosy, juicy, Lucy, sluicy; Debussy, Watusi.

-uid, druid, fluid.

-uilder, builder, gilder; guilder; bewilder, rebuilder.

-uilding, building, gilding; rebuilding.

-uin, bruin, ruin.

-uiser. See **-oser.**

-uitor. See **-ooter.**

-uker, euchre, fluker, lucre, puker; rebuker.

-uki. See **-ooky.**

-uky. See **-ooky.**

-ula, Beulah, hula, moola; tabbouleh, Talullah; Ashtabula, Boola Boola, hula-hula.

-ulep. See **-ulip.**

-ulgar, Bulgar, bulgur, vulgar.

-ulgence, effulgence, indulgence, refulgence; self-indulgence.

-ulgent, fulgent; effulgent, indulgent, refulgent; self-indulgent.

-ulip, julep, tulip.

-ulky, bulky, hulky, sulky.

-uller, color, cruller, culler, duller, guller, luller, sculler; annuller, discolor, medullar, off-color, tricolor; Technicolor, multicolor, watercolor.

-ullet (-o͞o-), bullet, pullet.

-ullet (-ul-), cullet, gullet, mullet.

-ulley. See **-ully.**

-ullion, cullion, mullion, scullion.

-ully (-o͞o-), bully, fully, pulley, woolly.

-ully (-ul-), cully, dully, gully, hully, sully, Tully.

-ulsion, pulsion; compulsion, convulsion, divulsion, emulsion, expulsion, impulsion, propulsion, repulsion, revulsion.

-ulsive, compulsive, convulsive, emulsive, expulsive, impulsive, propulsive, repulsive, revulsive.

-ultry, sultry; adultery.

-ulture, culture, vulture; agriculture, aviculture, floriculture, horticulture, pisciculture, viniculture.

-ulu, Lulu, Zulu; Honolulu.

-uly, coolie, coolly, coulee, Dooley, duly, Julie, newly, stoolie, Thule, truly; Bernoulli, patchouli, unduly, unruly; ultima Thule.

-uma, duma, puma, Yuma; mazuma; Montezuma.

-uman. See **-umen.**

-umbent, accumbent, decumbent, incumbent, procumbent, recumbent.

-umber, cumber, Humber, lumbar, lumber, number, slumber, umber; cucumber, encumber, outnumber; disencumber.

-umber. See **-ummer.**

-umble, bumble, crumble, fumble, grumble, humble, jumble, mumble, rumble, scumble, stumble, tumble, umbel.

-umbly, comely, dumbly, numbly.

-umbo, Dumbo, gumbo; mumbo-jumbo.

-umbrous, cumbrous, slumbrous; penumbrous.

-umby. See **-ummy.**

-umen, bloomin', crewman, human, lumen, Newman, Truman; acumen, albumin, bitumen, illumine, inhuman; catechumen, superhuman.

-umer, bloomer, boomer, fumer, humor, rumor, tumor; consumer, perfumer.

-umid, fumid, humid, tumid.

-umly. See **-umbly.**

-ummer, comer, drummer, dumber, hummer, mummer, number, plumber, scummer, summer; late-comer, midsummer, newcomer.

-ummit, plummet, summit.

-ummock. See **-omach.**

-ummy, crumby, crummy, dummy, gummy, lummy, mummy, plummy, rummy, scummy, slummy, thrummy, tummy, yummy.

-umnal, autumnal, columnal.

-umous, fumous, grumous, humus, spumous.

-umper, bumper, dumper, jumper, plumper, pumper, stumper, trumper, thumper.

-umpet, crumpet, strumpet, trumpet.

-umpish, dumpish, frumpish, grumpish, lumpish, plumpish.

-umpkin, bumpkin, lumpkin, pumpkin.

-umple, crumple, rumple.

-umption, gumption; assumption, consumption, presumption, resumption.

-umptious, bumptious, scrumptious; presumptious.

-umptive, assumptive, consumptive, presumptive, resumptive.

-umpus. See **-ompass.**

-umus. See **-umous.**

-una, luna, puna, tuna, Una; kahuna, lacuna, laguna, vicuna.

-unar. See **-uner.**

-uncheon, bruncheon, luncheon, puncheon, truncheon.

-unction, function, junction, unction; compunction, conjunction, disjunction, dysfunction, expunction, injunction.

-unctive, adjunctive, conjunctive, disjunctive, subjunctive.

-uncture, juncture, puncture; conjuncture.

-undance, abundance, redundance; superabundance.

-undant, abundant, redundant; superabundant.

-unday. See **-undy.**

-under, blunder, sunder, thunder, under, wonder; asunder, jocunder, refunder, rotunder, thereunder.

-undle, bundle, rundle, trundle.

-undy, Fundy, Grundy, Monday, Sunday, undie; Bay of Fundy, jaguarundi, Mrs. Grundy, salmagundi; coatimundi.

-uner, crooner, lunar, pruner, schooner, sooner, spooner, swooner, tuner; attuner, communer, harpooner, impugner, lacunar, oppugner; importuner.

-unger (-g-), hunger, monger, younger; fishmonger, gossipmonger, newsmonger; ironmonger.

-unger (-j-), blunger, lunger, plunger, sponger; expunger.

-ungle, bungle, jungle.

-unic, Munich, punic, Punic, runic, tunic.

-union. See **-onion.**

-unkard, bunkered, drunkard, Dunkard.

-unker, bunker, drunker, dunker, flunker, funker, junker, Junker, plunker, punker.

-unky, chunky, donkey, flunkey, funky, hunky, junky, monkey, spunky.

-unnage. See **-onnage.**

-unnel, funnel, gunwale, runnel, tunnel.

-unny, bunny, funny, gunny, honey, money, sonny, sunny, Tunney, tunny.

-untal. See **-untle.**

-unter, blunter, bunter, grunter, hunter, punter; confronter.

-untle, frontal, gruntle; disgruntle; contrapuntal.

-unwale. See **-unnel.**

-uoy. See **-ewy.**

-upboard, blubbered, cupboard, Hubbard, rubbered.

-uper. See **-ooper.**

-upil. See **-uple.**

-uple, pupil; scruple, octuple, quadruple, quintuple, septuple, sextuple.

-uplet, drupelet; octuplet, quadruplet, quintuplet, septuplet, sextuplet.

-upor. See **-ooper.**

-upper, crupper, scupper, supper, upper.

-upple. See **-ouple.**

-uppy, guppy, puppy, yuppie.

-ura, pleura; bravura, caesura; Angostura; coloratura; appoggiatura.

-ural, crural, jural, mural, neural, pleural, plural, rural, Ural; intermural, intramural, sinecural.

-urance, durance; assurance, endurance, insurance; reassurance.

-urban, bourbon, Durban, turban, urban; exurban, suburban; interurban.

-urchin. See **-irchen.**

-urder, girder, herder, murder; absurder, engirder, sheepherder.

-urdle. See **-irdle.**

-urdly. See **-irdly.**

-urdy, birdie, sturdy, wordy; hurdy-gurdy.

-urely, purely; demurely, maturely, obscurely, securely.

-urement, abjurement, allurement, immurement, obscurement, procurement.

-urer, curer, führer, furor, juror, lurer, purer; abjuror, insurer, nonjuror, procurer, securer.

-urgate, expurgate, objurgate.

-urgence. See **-ergence.**

-urgent. See **-ergent.**

-urgeon, burgeon, sturgeon, surgeon, virgin.

-urger. See **-erger.**

-urgle, burgle, gurgle.

-urgy, clergy, dirgy, surgy; liturgy; dramaturgy, metallurgy, thaumaturgy.

-uric, purpuric, sulfuric, telluric.

-urist, jurist, purist, tourist; manicurist; caricaturist, miniaturist.

-urker. See **-irker.**

-urky. See **-erky.**

-urler, burler, curler, furler, hurler, purler, skirler, twirler, whirler.

-urlew, curlew, purlieu.

-urling, curling, furling, hurling, purling, skirling, sterling, swirling, twirling, whirling; uncurling.

-urlish. See **-irlish.**

-urloin, purloin, sirloin.

-urly, burly, churly, curly, early, girlie, hurly,

knurly, pearly, Shirley, squirrely, surly,
swirly, twirly, whirly; hurly-burly.

-urma, Burma, derma, Irma; terra firma.

-urmese. See **-ermes.**

-urmur. See **-irmer.**

-urnal. See **-ernal.**

-urner. See **-earner.**

-urning. See **-earning.**

-urnish, burnish, furnish.

-uror. See **-urer.**

-urper, burper, chirper; usurper.

-urrage. See **-ourage.**

-urrish. See **-ourish.**

-urro. See **-orough.**

-urrow. See **-orough.**

-urry, burry, curry, flurry, furry, hurry,
scurry, slurry, surrey, worry.

-ursal. See **-ersal.**

-urser, bursar, cursor, mercer, nurser,
purser; disburser, precursor.

-ursor. See **-urser.**

-urtain. See **-ertain.**

-urter. See **-erter.**

-urtive. See **-ertive.**

-urtle fertile, hurtle, kirtle, myrtle, Myrtle,
turtle, whirtle; infertile.

-urtly. See **-ertly.**

-urvant. See **-ervant.**

-urvy, curvy, nervy, scurvy; topsy-turvy.

-ury (-o͞o-), Curie, fleury, fury, Fury, houri,
Jewry, jury; Missouri; de jure, potpourri,
tandoori.

-ury (-e-). See **-erry.**

-usa, Sousa, Medusa; Arethusa; lollapalooza.

-usal. See **-oozle.**

-uscan, buskin, dusken, Ruskin, Tuscan; Etruscan, molluscan.

-uscle. See **-ustle.**

-usel. See **-oozle.**

-user, user; abuser, accuser, amuser, diffuser, excuser. See also **-oser.**

-usher, blusher, brusher, crusher, flusher, gusher, husher, plusher, rusher, usher; four-flusher.

-ushy, gushy, mushy, plushy, slushy.

-usi. See **-uicy.**

-usier. See **-izzier.**

-usion, fusion; allusion, Carthusian, collusion, conclusion, confusion, contusion, delusion, diffusion, effusion, elusion, exclusion, extrusion, illusion, inclusion, infusion, intrusion, Malthusian, obtrusion, occlusion, profusion, protrusion, reclusion, seclusion, suffusion, transfusion; disillusion, interfusion.

-usive, abusive, allusive, collusive, conclusive, conducive, delusive, diffusive, effusive, exclusive, illusive, inclusive, infusive, intrusive, obtrusive, reclusive, seclusive; inconclusive.

-uskin, buskin, Ruskin.

-usky, dusky, husky, musky.

-uso, Crusoe, Rousseau, trousseau, whoso; Caruso.

-ussel. See **-ustle.**

-usset, gusset, russet.

-ussia, Prussia, Russia.

-ussian. See **-ussion.**

-ussion, Prussian, Russian; concussion, discussion, percussion; repercussion.

-ussive, concussive, discussive, percussive; repercussive.

-ussy, fussy, Gussie, hussy, mussy.

-ustard, blustered, bustard, clustered, custard, flustered, mustard, mustered.

-uster, bluster, buster, cluster, Custer, duster, fluster, juster, luster, muster, thruster, truster; adjuster, lackluster; filibuster.

-ustered. See **-ustard.**

-ustic, fustic, rustic.

-ustion, fustian; combustion.

-ustle, bustle, hustle, justle, muscle, mussel, rustle, tussle.

-ustler, bustler, hustler, rustler, tussler.

-ustly, justly; augustly, robustly, unjustly.

-usty, busty, crusty, dusty, gusty, lusty, musty, rusty, trusty.

-usy. See **-izzy.**

-utal, brutal, tootle; refutal.

-uter. See **-ooter.**

-utest. See **-utist.**

-uthful, ruthful, truthful, youthful; untruthful.

-uthless, ruthless, toothless, truthless.

-utie. See **-ooty.**

-utile, futile; inutile.

-ution, Lucian; ablution, Aleutian, Confucian, dilution, locution, pollution, solution, volution; absolution, attribution, comminution, constitution, contribution, convolution, destitution, devolution, diminution, dissolution, distribution, elocution, evolution, execution, institution, involution, Lilliputian, persecution, prosecution, prostitution, resolution, restitution, retribution, revolution, Rosicrucian, substitution; circumlocution, electrocution, irresolution, reconstitution, redistribution.

-utist, cutest, flutist, lutist; pharmaceutist, therapeutist.

-utive, coadjutive, constitutive, diminutive, persecutive, resolutive.

-utler, butler, cutler, scuttler, subtler.

-utor. See **-ooter.**

-uttal. See **-uttle.**

-utter, butter, clutter, cutter, flutter, gutter, mutter, putter, shutter, splutter, sputter, strutter, stutter, utter; abutter, rebutter, stonecutter, woodcutter.

-uttish, ruttish, sluttish.

-uttle, buttle, cuttle, scuttle, shuttle, subtle; rebuttal.

-uttler. See **-utler.**

-utton, button, glutton, mutton; bachelor button.

-utty, nutty, puttee, putty, rutty, smutty.

-uture, future, moocher, suture.

-uty. See **-ooty.**

-uxion. See **-uction.**

-uyer. See **-ier.**

-uzzle, guzzle, muzzle, nuzzle, puzzle.

-uzzler, guzzler, muzzler, nuzzler, puzzler.

-uzzy, fuzzy, muzzy, scuzzy, fuzzy-wuzzy.

-yan. See **-ion.**

-yer. See **-ier.**

-ylla. See **-illa.**

-ylon, nylon, pylon, trylon.

-yly. See **-ily.**

-ymbal. See **-imble.**

-ymbol. See **-imble.**

-ymic. See **-imic.**

-yming. See **-iming.**

-yncher. See **-incher.**

-yness. See **-inus.**

-ynic. See **-inic.**

-ypsy, gypsy, ipse, tipsy; Poughkeepsie.

-yptic, cryptic, diptych, glyptic, styptic, trip-tych; ecliptic, elliptic; apocalyptic.

-yra. See **-ira.**

-yrant. See **-irant.**

-yrate, gyrate, irate, lyrate; circumgyrate.

-yric, lyric, Pyrrhic; butyric, empiric, satiric, satyric; panegyric.

-yron. See **-iren.**

-yrtle. See **-urtle.**

-yrus. See **-irus.**

-ysian. See **-ision.**

-ysic, phthisic, physic; metaphysic.

-ysmal. See **-ismal.**

-yssal. See **-istle.**

-ystic. See **-istic.**

-ytic. See **-itic.**

Glossary of Poetic Terms

accent, the stress or emphasis placed on certain syllables, usually indicated by a mark (´) above the stressed syllable. An unaccented syllable is usually indicated by a short mark (˘) above the syllable. Example:

Had wĕ but wŏrld ĕnoúgh, ănd tíme

alexandrine (al´ig zan´drin), a line of verse consisting of six iambic feet. Example:

Ăll clád | ĭn Lín|cŏln gréen, | wĭth cáps | ŏf réd | ănd blúe |

alliteration, the repetition of the same consonant sound or sound group, especially in initial stressed syllables. Example:

The *s*oft *s*weet *s*ound of *S*ylvia's voice

amphibrach (am´fə brak´), a foot consisting of an unaccented syllable followed by an accented and an unaccented syllable. Example (the first three feet are amphibrachs):

Thĕ cláns ăre | ĭmpá tiĕnt | ănd chíde thy̆ | dĕláy

amphimacer (am fim´ə sər), a foot consisting of an accented syllable followed by an unaccented syllable and an accented syllable. Example:

Cátch ă stár, | fálling fást |

anapest (an´ə pest´), a foot consisting of two unaccented syllables followed by one accented syllable. The adjective form is *anapestic*. Example:

Nĕvĕr héar | thĕ swĕet mú|sĭc ŏf spéech |

assonance, the use of identical vowel sounds in several words, often as a substitute for rhyme. Example:

> Shrink his thin essence like a riveled flow'r

ballad, **1.** a simple narrative poem of popular origin, composed in short stanzas, often of a romantic nature and adapted for singing. **2.** any poem written in such a style.

ballade (bə läd´, ba-), a poem consisting (usually) of three stanzas having an identical rhyme scheme, followed by an envoy. The final line of each stanza and the envoy are the same.

ballad stanza, a four-line stanza in which the first and third lines are in iambic tetrameter while the second and fourth lines are in iambic trimeter; the second and fourth lines rhyme. In a common variant, the alternate lines rhyme. Example:

> They followed from the snowy bank
> Those footsteps one by one,
> Into the middle of the plank—
> And further there was none.

blank verse, unrhymed verse in iambic pentameter, usually not in formal stanza units. Example:

> Fair seed|time had | my soul, | and I | grew up
> Fostered | alike | by beau|ty and | by fear
> Much fa|vored in | my birth|place, and | no less
> In that | belov|èd Vale | to which | erelong
> We were | transplant|ed...

caesura (si zhŏor′ə), the main pause in a line of verse, usually near the middle. Example:

> Know then thyself, ‖ presume not God to scan

cinquain (sing kān′), a stanza consisting of five lines.

consonance, the use of an identical pattern of consonants in different words. Examples:

> time – tome – team – tame
> fall – fell – fill – full
> slow – slew – slay – sly

closed couplet, a couplet whose sense is completed within its two lines. Example:

> True wit is nature to advantage dress'd
> What oft was thought, but ne'er so well express'd

couplet, two consecutive lines that rhyme. Example:

> Touch her not scornfully;
> Think of her mournfully

dactyl (dak′til), a foot consisting of one accented syllable followed by two unaccented syllables. The adjective form is *dactylic.* Example:

> Cánnŏn tŏ | right ŏf thĕm |

dimeter (dim′i tər), a line of verse consisting of two feet.

distich (dis′tik), a couplet.

elegy, a subjective, meditative poem, especially one that expresses grief or sorrow.

enjambment (en jam′mənt). See **run-on line.**

envoy (en′voi), **1.** a short stanza concluding a poem in certain archaic metrical forms. **2.** a postscript to a poetical composition, sometimes serving as a dedication.

epic, a long narrative poem about persons of heroic stature and actions of great significance, and conforming to a rigid organization and form. Examples are the *Iliad* and the *Odyssey* of Homer, Virgil's *Aeneid, Beowulf,* and Milton's *Paradise Lost.*

epigram, a short and pithy remark, often in verse.

feminine ending, an ending on a word in which the final syllable is unaccented. Examples:

softness, careful, another, fairest

foot, the metrical unit in poetry, consisting of one accented syllable and one or more unaccented syllables. The most commonly found feet are the **iamb,** the **anapest,** the **dactyl,** and the **trochee.** The foot is usually marked in scansion by a vertical line. Example:

Ĭ am mŏn|arch of all | Ĭ survey |

free verse, verse that does not adhere to a fixed pattern of meter, rhyme, or other poetic conventions. Example:

The sea is calm tonight.
The tide is full, the moon lies fair
Upon the straits; on the French coast the light
Gleams and is gone; the cliffs of England stand,
Glimmering and vast, out in the tranquil bay.

heptameter (hep tam′i tər), a line of verse consisting of seven feet.

heroic couplet, two consecutive rhyming lines in iambic pentameter. Example:

> O thoughtless mortals! Ever blind to fate,
> Too soon dejected, and too soon elate.

hexameter (hek sam′i tər), a line of verse consisting of six feet.

iamb (ī′am), a foot consisting of one unaccented syllable followed by one accented syllable. The iamb is the most common metrical foot in English verse because it fits the natural pattern of English words. The adjective form is *iambic.* Example:

> The cur|few tolls | the knell | of part|ing day. |

Following is an example of *iambic pentameter:*

> Shall I | compare | thee to | a sum|mer's day?
> Thou art | more love|ly and | more tem|perate:
> Rough winds | do shake | the dar|ling buds | of
>   May,
> And sum|mer's lease | hath all | too short | a
>   date...

internal rhyme, a rhyme that occurs within a line. Example:

> So *slight* the *light*
> I could not see
> My *fair,* dear *Clair,*
> That it was thee.

Italian sonnet, a sonnet written in iambic pentameter with a rhyme scheme of *abba abba cde dde*. There are occasional variants of the rhyme scheme in the last six lines. The first eight lines (the *octave*) usually present a theme or premise; the last six lines (the *sestet*) present the conclusion or resolution. Also called **Petrarchan sonnet** after the 14th-century Italian poet.

limerick, a five-line poem using trimeters for the first, second, and fifth lines, and using dimeters for the third and fourth lines. It is usually written in a mixture of amphibrachs and iambs.

lyric, a poem with a particularly musical, songlike quality.

macaronic verse (mak′ə ron′ik), verse in which two or more languages are interlaced.

masculine ending, an ending on a word in which the final syllable is accented. Examples:

> resound, avoid, reply, consume

meter, the basic rhythmic description of a line in terms of its accented and unaccented syllables. Meter describes the sequence and relationship of all the syllables of a line. Examples of meter are *iambic pentameter* and *dactylic hexameter*.

monometer (mə nom′i tər), a line of verse consisting of one foot.

octave, the first eight lines of an Italian sonnet.

octometer (ok tom′i tər), a line of verse consisting of eight feet.

ode, a poem, usually complicated in its metrical and stanzaic form, on a highly serious or particularly important theme.

onomatopoeia (on′ə mat′ə pē′ə), the quality of a word that imitates the sound it designates. Examples:

honk, bang, tintinnabulation

ottava rima (ō tä′və rē′mə), a stanza written in iambic pentameter with a rhyme scheme of *abababcc.*

pastoral, a poem dealing with simple rural life.

pentameter (pen tam′i tər), a line of verse consisting of five feet.

Petrarchan sonnet. See **Italian sonnet.**

quatrain (kwo′trān), a stanza consisting of four lines.

refrain, an expression, a line, or a group of lines that is repeated at certain points in a poem, usually at the end of a stanza.

rhyme, an identity of certain sounds in different words, usually the last words in two or more lines.

rhyme royal, a stanza written in iambic pentameter with a rhyme scheme of *ababbcc.*

rhyme scheme, the pattern of rhyme used in a stanza or poem. Rhyme scheme is indicated with letters: *abab, cdcd, abba, cddc,* etc. An example of *ababcc* rhyme scheme is:

I wandered lonely as a cloud	*a*
That floats on high o'er vales and hills,	*b*
When all at once I saw a crowd,	*a*
A host, of golden daffodils;	*b*
Beside the lake, beneath the trees,	*c*
Fluttering and dancing in the breeze.	*c*

rondeau (ron′dō), a poem consisting of three stanzas of five, three, and five lines, using only two rhymes throughout. A refrain appears at the end of the second and third stanzas.

rondel (ron′dl), a poem consisting (usually) of fourteen lines on two rhymes, of which four are made up of the initial couplet repeated in the middle and at the end (the second line of the couplet sometimes being omitted at the end).

rondelet (ron′dl et′), a poem consisting of five lines on two rhymes, the opening word or words being used after the second and fifth lines as an unrhymed refrain.

run-on line, a line of verse having a thought that carries over to the next line without a pause. Also called **enjambment.**

scansion, the process of indicating the pattern of accented and unaccented syllables in a line of verse.

septet, a stanza consisting of seven lines.

sestet, a group of six lines, especially those at the end of a sonnet.

sestina (se stē′nə), a poem of six six-line stanzas and a three-line envoy, originally without rhyme, in which each stanza repeats the end words of the lines of the first stanza, but in different order. The envoy uses these six end words again, three in the middle of the lines and three at the end.

Shakespearean sonnet, a sonnet written in iambic pentameter with a rhyme scheme of *abab cdcd efef gg.* The theme is often presented in the three quatrains, and the poem is concluded with the couplet.

sight rhyme, not a rhyme but two or more words which end in identical spelling. Examples:

> though, bough, through

slant rhyme, an approximate rhyme, usually characterized by assonance or consonance.

song, a short and simple poem, usually suitable for setting to music.

sonnet, a poem consisting of fourteen lines in iambic pentameter. The most common forms are the **Italian sonnet** and the **Shakespearean sonnet.**

Spenserian stanza, a stanza consisting of eight iambic pentameter lines and a final iambic hexameter line, with a rhyme scheme of *ababbcbcc*. The Spenserian stanza is named after the 16th-century English poet, Edmund Spenser.

spondee (spon′dē), a foot consisting of two accented syllables. Example:

Spéak sóft, | stánd stíll |

stanza, a fixed pattern of lines or rhymes, or both.

stress. See **accent.**

tercet (tûr′sit), a group of three consecutive lines that rhyme together or relate to an adjacent tercet by rhymes.

terza rima (tert′sə rē′mə), a poem in iambic meter consisting of eleven-syllable lines arranged in tercets, the middle line of each tercet rhyming with the first and third lines of the following tercet. Dante's *Divine Comedy* is written in terza rima.

tetrameter (te tram′i tər), a line of verse consisting of four feet.

trimeter (trim′i tər), a line of verse consisting of three feet.

triolet (trē′ə lā′), an eight-line stanza in which line 1 recurs as line 4 and line 7, while line 2 recurs as line 8.

triplet, a stanza consisting of three lines.

trochee (trō′kē), a foot consisting of one accented syllable followed by one unaccented syllable. The adjective form is *trochaic.* Example:

> Why so | pále and | wán fond | lóver
> Príthee, | whý so | pále?

vers de société (ver də sô syā tā′), a light-spirited and witty poem, usually brief, dealing with some social fashion or foible.

verse, 1. one line of a poem. **2.** a group of lines in a poem. **3.** any form in which rhythm is regularized.

villanelle (vil′ə nel′), a poem consisting of (usually) five tercets and a final quatrain, using only two rhymes throughout.

weak rhyme, rhyme which falls upon the unaccented (or lightly accented) syllables.

Notes